# The British Garrison

# Berlin

# 1945 - 1994

"nowhere to go . . . ."

A pictorial historiography
of the
British Military presence in Berlin 1945 - 1994

Bibliografische Informationen der Deutschen Nationalbibliothek
Die Deutsche Nationalbibliothek verzeichnet diese
Publikation in der Deutschen Nationalbibliografie;
detaillierte bibliografische Daten sind im Internet über
http://dnb.d-nb.de abrufbar.

ISBN: 978-3-86408-068-5
© Copyright: Vergangenheitsverlag, Berlin / 2012

www.vergangenheitsverlag.de

Alle Rechte, auch die des Nachdrucks von Auszügen,
der fotomechanischen und digitalen Wiedergabe
und der Übersetzung, vorbehalten.

# The British Garrison

# BERLIN

## 1945 - 1994.

"nowhere to go . . . ."

William Durie.
wd@photo-durie.com
Copyright Lives.

This book is dedicated to the men and women of the United Kingdom and Commonwealth Armed Forces who served in Berlin from 1945 to 1994 and to the people of West Berlin who in times of tension and uncertainty stood steadfast with their British Ally.

*We are all survivors of the cold war.*

The photographs, documents, text and graphics reproduced in this book are copyright protected. Reproduction in present media or media still to be developed is only permitted with the written consent of the author or the copyright holder. Unauthorised reproductions could result in legal action being taken.

Copyright 2011.
Copyright Lives.

Text edited: Maj. Gen. (Retd) Sir Robert Corbett, KCVO, CB.
& Sven Duncan Durie.
Layout: wd@photo-durie.com

# Contents.

| | | | |
|---|---|---|---|
| **Forward.** | 3 | **Quadripartite control:** | 50 - 61 |
| Maj. Gen. (Retd) Sir Robert Corbett | | Control Council. | 51 |
| **Preface.** | 4 | Victory parades. | 52 -53 |
| | | Berlin Document Centre. | 54 - 55 |
| **The `Zitadelle´, Berlin 1945:** | 5 - 7 | Spandau prison. | 56 - 58 |
| Trümmerfrauen. | 6 | Berlin Air Safety Centre. | 59 - 61 |
| Declaration of Legality. | 7 | | |
| | | **The Kommandatura:** | 62 - 72 |
| **British Military Government, Berlin Area:** | 8 - 18 | Tripartite control. | 64 |
| Entry to Berlin. | 9 | Allied Staff Berlin. | 65 |
| Headquarters Berlin. | 10 -11 | Tripartite exercises. | 66 - 67 |
| Establishing control. | 12 | Civil Defence. | 68 - 69 |
| Prime Minister Churchill in Berlin. | 13 | Allied Forces Day parade. | 70 - 71 |
| Fraternisation. | 14 - 15 | Allied weapons meeting. | 72 |
| Black market. | 16 | | |
| Der-Berliner. | 17 | **Brothers in arms, the Soviets:** | 73 - 81 |
| Potsdam conference. | 18 | Soviet war memorial. | 74 - 76 |
| | | Severing links. | 77 |
| **Combat Arms:** | 19 - 49 | Loophole. | 78 |
| Preparing for war. | 20 - 21 | Uprising, Voting with their feet. | 79 |
| March and shoot. | 22 - 23 | Flag tours. | 80 |
| Rocking Horses. | 24 - 25 | Liaison with the Soviets. | 81 |
| Skill at arms. | 27 | | |
| Women to arms. | 28 | **The silent dual (the intelligence war):** | 82 - 106 |
| Territorial Army. | 30 | British Military Liaison Mission. | 83 - 92 |
| London - Berlin. | 31 | Spies among us. | 93 |
| Fit-to-Fight. | 32 | Operation ´PBJOINTLY´. | 94 - 98 |
| Driver training. | 34 | Spy in the sky. | 99 |
| More fire power. | 35 | Fieldstation `Teufelsberg´. | 100 - 103 |
| Wall and wire patrols. | 36 - 37 | Yak - 28P incident. | 104 |
| Berlin Military Tattoo. | 38 - 40 | East Berlin military parades. | 106 |
| Protocol visits. | 42 - 43 | | |
| Public relations. | 44 - 45 | **Allied access:** | 107 - 116 |
| Sport. | 47 | Access agreement. | 108 |
| Local employed labour. | 48 - 49 | Overland corridor. | 109 - 111 |
| | | British Military Train. | 112 - 116 |

| | | | |
|---|---|---|---|
| **Crisis in East Berlin:** | 117 - 122 | ***"Immediately",* 9 November 1989:** | 165 - 168 |
| Closing the loophole. | 118 | Maj. Gen. Corbett, at the Wall. | 166 |
| Checkpoint Charlie (C). | 119 | Hammers and chisels. | 167 |
| Living with the Wall. | 120 - 121 | Opening of the Brandenburg Gate. | 168 |
| Wall encounters. | 122 | | |
| | | **Re-unification - The draw-down:** | 169 - 173 |
| **Defending its sector, "nowhere to go . . . .":** | 123 - 139 | 2+4 - Agreement. | 170 |
| | | Goodbye Charlie. | 171 |
| Fighting in Built up Area. | 125 - 126 | A Museum to the Allies. | 172 - 173 |
| Obstacle zone, `shoot and scoot´. | 127 | Farewell parade. | 174 |
| Delay zone of combat. | 128 | Everyone has a suitcase in Berlin. | 175 |
| Yellow pages. | 129 | | |
| Final defence zone of combat. | 131 | **British Commandants, 1945 to 1990.** | 176 - 177 |
| Lessons learnt. | 132 - 133 | | |
| Workshops' role. | 134 - 135 | **Brigade Commanders, 1950 to 1994.** | 178 |
| Battle tanks in FIBUA. | 136 | | |
| Urban camouflage, | 137 | **Deputy Commandants, 1961 to 1990.** | 178 |
| Logistic in FIBUA. | 138 | | |
| Dumping to task. | 139 | **Roll of call of British units that served in Berlin, 1945 to 1994.** | 179 - 180 |
| **Royal Air Force, Gatow:** | 140 - 146 | | |
| The early days. | 141 | **Sources.** | 180 |
| Finest hour. | 142 - 146 | | |
| | | **Index.** | 181 - 183 |
| **Royalty comes to Berlin:** | 147 - 151 | | |
| Royal standard. | 148 | **Chronology.** | 184 - 187 |
| Queen's Birthday Parade. | 149 | | |
| Royal visitors. | 150 | **Acknowledgements.** | 187 |
| Colonel-in-Chief. | 151 | | |
| **Brigade's infrastructure:** | 152 - 164 | | |
| Barracks. | 153 - 154 | | |
| Villa Lemm, Edinburgh House. | 155 | | |
| Gatow Ranges. | 156 | | |
| British Military Hospital. | 157 | | |
| NAAFI Club. | 158 - 159 | | |
| Berlin war cemetery. | 160 | | |
| British Berlin Yacht Club. | 161 | | |
| B. F. B. S. | 162 | | |
| St. George's church and hall | 163 | | |
| British Centre, Toc-H club. | 164 | | |

# Forward

**21 years** ago, on 3 October 1990, the first day of German Unity, I left RAF Gatow with my Wife having completed my duties as 21st and last Commandant of the British Sector of Berlin. At midnight on 2/3 October we had stood with President von Weizsacker, Chancellor Kohl and other distinguished Germans on the dais in front of the Reichstag Parliament Building. Together we had watched as the throng of over a million people, assembled in the open ground below while the German flag was raised, for the first time in Berlin since the ending of the Second World War, tumultuously sang the National Hymn. As we walked back into the magnificently restored Reichstag Building - which I had first seen in ruins as a young Platoon Commander in 1961 at the start of the Wall - I sought to congratulate the Chancellor on this great day for his people, to which he replied, " Commandant, we could never have done it without you Allies". Nor could we, for our part, ever imagined these dramatic moments, nor those heady and often very complicated days which, following President Gorbachev's visit to East Berlin the previous October, had begun so utterly to change the world. And the key to these seismic changes had undoubtedly lain with divided Berlin, front line city of the Cold War.

The British garrison, who in July 1945 had come to Berlin as conquerors and had, through the 1948 Airlift, so rapidly become protectors - Schutzmachte - and then friends, achieving in the process one of the most remarkable examples of reconciliation in history, played an indispensable role in safeguarding this bastion of freedom surrounded by a hostile communist sea. Together with its US and French comrades, this garrison of British soldiers and airmen, most admirably supported by its diplomats and by the West Berliners, had stood steadfast in Berlin through four and a half sometimes very difficult decades. In 1994 it could finally withdraw from the City with the satisfaction of knowing that it had played an unique role in making of post-war European history.

William Durie's excellent book portrays this story graphically. He reminds us that what happened in 1989/90 could not, in the final analysis, have been achieved without the dedication and service of the Allied garrisons in Berlin. This should be an enduring source of genuine pride. By his work, Willie will help to ensure that this is the case. He is to be commended for it.

7 January 2012.

Major General (Retd) Sir Robert Corbett, KCVO, CB
21st. and last Commandant of the British Sector, Berlin.

**Preface.**

**Berlin** is the largest city between Paris and Moscow. Legend has it that 'Bärlin' was founded by Albert the Bear, Margrave of Brandenburg, on the site where he witnessed a she-bear playing with her cubs. The story is reflected in the city's coat of arms, which has since early times depicted a bear. Over the centuries, the bear has come to symbolize the strength and virtues shown by the people of Berlin in times of adversity. Few times were more demanding than the turbulent and unsettling years of the post-war era, during which the city, in one way, returned to its roots as a divided settlement on either side of the River Spree.
The city which was later to become the capital of the German Empire, began as two separate towns, Berlin and Cölln. Although both towns had prehistoric roots, it was not until 1237 that one of them, Cölln, was first given a written mention. By 1307 both townships had united for defence and continued to prosper under this alliance. However, in the fifteenth century the union was dissolved. Although its history dates from the early part of the 13th century, Berlin was in 1939 a thoroughly modern city, capital of both the Reich and Prussia. Berlin was the second largest metropolis on the continent and the fifth largest in the world. According to the 1944 World Almanac, it had a population of 4,322,242 souls, but war casualties and the exodus of an unknown number of refugees from American and British air raids reduced the population considerably. Current estimates, based upon food ration cards issued in 1944, indicate a civilian population of about 3,000,000, of whom 280,000 lived in the British sector.

During World War Two, the city came under fire. After sporadic bombings of Berlin during the years 1940 and 1941, the systematic destruction of the various quarters of the city began in the year 1943. By early 1944 Allied bombers were levelling Berlin's buildings using incendiaries and high explosives. At this time, the Red Army was beginning its tidal wave across Northwest Germany. Berlin faced imminent capture by late April 1945. After encircling the town from all sides (except gaps to the west and northwest) the Soviets made their main attack from the east and north. By the end of the month, they had closed in and had begun unleashing infantry, tanks and artillery along the main thoroughfares.

On 2 May 1945, after one of the most intense battles in human history, the guns stopped firing amongst the ruins of Berlin. Less than four years after his attack on the Soviet Union, Hitler's self-proclaimed thousand-year Reich had ceased to exist. But the human costs of the Battle for Berlin had been enormous. Millions of shells had been fired into a city that was already devastated after two years of relentless bombing raids by British and American warplanes. Nearly a quarter of a million people died during the last three weeks of World War Two. Europe would never be the same again. Despite Cold War tensions, the continent would remain free of war for decades to come - something unprecedented in European history.

The Americans and British joined the Soviets in Berlin on 4 July, followed by the French on 12 August. As early as 12 September 1944, the Four Powers had agreed on military administration of Germany after the war and their proposals were put into practice. The country was divided into four zones of occupation: The Americans, British and French occupied their respective regions of what would become the Federal Republic of Germany (West Germany), and the Soviets held onto that part of Germany which they had captured and which would become the German Democratic Republic (East Germany). Though well inside the Soviet zone of occupied Germany, Berlin as the capital city was afforded a special status and was subdivided into four sectors administrated by the Four Powers. Berlin was not considered to be part of the Soviet zone.

Until Germany's unification on 3 October 1990, the Western Allies and the Soviets, with their diametrically opposed systems, confronted one another in the divided city. Since 1945 Berlin had played a dominant part in international events, it had been at the centre of major international crises on three occasions. Berlin's security was guarantee by the presence of the American, British and French garrisons and upheld by undisputed legal rights, The Declaration of Legality, signed on 5 June 1945, had sustained the freedom of two million inhabitants in West Berlin since 1945.

After 49 years of presence in Berlin, British forces together with their US and French Allies having gained a bloodless victory over the communist, witnessing the break-up of the Warsaw Pact, and having successfully completed a four year draw down programme officially withdrew from Berlin on 8 September 1994.

## The `Zitadelle´, Berlin 1945.

**In** the concluding stages of World War Two, the remains of the German Army, still in Berlin and fit-to-fight, were concentrated in the city's central defence sector `Die-Zitadelle´. The sector was bounded by the Landwehr-Canal and the river Spree with external bastions as far as the Knie (Ernst-Reuter-Platz) in the west and Alexanderplatz in the east. This area contained government buildings, Adolf Hitler's bunker, the Swiss Embassy, the Brandenburg Gate, the Reichstag and the Defence Headquarters of Major General Mohnke with more than half a division of various Waffen-SS units under his direct command. The Brandenburg Gate and the Reichstag, although of no strategic value, were seen by the Soviets as symbols of Hitler's hated Germany. Both buildings were severely damaged in the last days and hours of fierce fighting between an encircled German Army, with nowhere to run and a Soviet Army seeking revenge.

After vicious battles had been waged, not only for every single building but for every room, basement and stairway, in intense house-to-house fighting in the city's suburbs, the Soviets gradually squeezed in on the final bastion of German resistance in Berlin `Die-Zitadelle´.

The Soviet wartime leader Joseph Stalin had let it be known to his field commanders that he expected the red hammer and sickle flag to be hoisted above the Reichstag in time for the forth coming May Day celebrations. After a number of attempts to storm the Reichstag had been beaten back by the defenders, and with time running out, the Soviets decided to wait for the cover of darkness before launching a final assault on 30 April at 1800 hours. Once the news got back that the leading troops had smashed their way into the building by firing two trench mortars held horizontally, a picked team with a special red banner rushed forward and managed to fight its way to the rear of the building where they found a staircase leading up to a parapet overlooking the Brandenburg Gate. The banner was hoisted 70 minutes before Stalin's deadline. With Adolf Hitler and his successor Joseph Goebbels both having committed suicide, General of Artillery Weidling, the military commander of the city, surrendered to Marshall Zukhov on 2 May at 1300 hours at Tempelhof. Zukhov later received the honour of being the `Conqueror of Berlin´. According to Soviet veterans, the silence that followed the fighting was literally deafening.

The battle for the Reichstag had cost the Germans 2,500 and the Soviets 2,200 lives. Shortly before the surrender, Waffen SS units aware of their fate at Soviet hands, took advantage of the darkness to break out of Berlin and head west to the German lines near the river Elbe. Only a handful reached the Elbe, the majority were wiped out by the Soviets rear cordon of steel which had been specially deployed to capture escaping high-ranking Nazi-government officials. The Soviets losses for the Battle for Berlin are estimated at some 70,000 dead.

The `Zitadelle´, Berlin 1945 - Trümmerfrau

**When** the Soviet army entered Berlin on 20 April 1945, Adolf Hitler's fifty-sixth and last birthday, it came face to face with the reality of modern war. American and British bombing raids combined with Soviet ground fire had destroyed and scarred the city beyond recognition.

**The** Soviets having plundered the cities heavy plant equipment and with a shortage of able men it was the women, Trümmerfrauen, from all walks of society who for a hourly rate of 0,72 Reichsmarks and a Grade II ration card physically cleared and helped to rebuilt the city.

The `Zitadelle´, Berlin 1945 - Declaration of Legality

**For** the signing of the Declaration of Legality in Berlin on 5 June 1945 the Soviet Commandant, Major General Bersarin, ordered that the flags of America, Britain, France and the Soviet Union be hoisted on public buildings. With a scarcity of materials the manufactured flags came in all shapes, colours and sizes.

**Representing** and signing the Declaration of Legality on behalf of their governments in Berlin were: from left to right, for the Soviet Union Marshal Zhukov, General of the Army Eisenhower for America and Field Marshal Montgomery for Great Britain and its Commonwealth.

## British Military Government, Berlin Area.

**For** nearly three months, the Soviets had ruled Berlin alone. Then, in accordance with the Yalta Agreement, troops from Britain and America arrived to take over their occupation sectors. A British reconnaissance party left Wolfenbüttel in the British zone at 0430 hours on 1 July and eventually reach Berlin at 1700 hours by a circuitous route, after being blocked by the Soviets at the motorway bridge over the river Elbe near Magdeburg. An advance party which was to be known as the 'British Military Government, Berlin Area', followed a day later under the command of Brigadier Hinde. The 7th Armoured Division (Desert Rats), who made up the main body with detachments from services and augmented by the 1st Battalion Grenadier Guards under the command of the first British Commandant and GOC, Major General Lewis Lyne, reached Berlin on 4 July. The British like the Americans were faced with a political `fait accompli´. In their sole occupation of Berlin from April to July, the Soviets had secured complete control of the city and its political structure. They had on 14 May 1945 appointed a municipal council for Greater Berlin. Key administrative positions, such as the police presidency, were held by Soviet-trained Germans bound to the Stalinist party, a number of whom had spent the war in exile in Moscow. The Berlin Radio station, although in the British sector, was under Soviet supervision and clocks ran on Moscow time. At a meeting with the Soviet military commandant on 11 July it was agreed that the British would take responsibility for their sector.

On 12 July, at 0900 hours, six British teams took over control from the German administration, set up by the Soviets in the administrative districts of Charlottenburg, Reinickendorf, Spandau, Tiergarten and Wilmersdorf. The tasks of the British teams were to establish control of an already functioning administration and to assert British authority in face of officials, who were originally appointed by the Soviets and still either bound in gratitude or in fear of them, asking for Soviet permission before obeying British orders. The British group responsible for the military government of Berlin functioned initially under the Director of Military Government at 21 Army Group. Over the following months, the field organisation altered from a body being exclusively military to one of predominantly civil character.

At the meeting on 11 July, the Soviets demanded that the British were to provide food and coal for their sector. From July 1945 to April 1946, the British supplied over 400,000 tons of food to Berlin. This was at a cost of around 30 million pounds; a serious problem at a time when Britain was on lower than wartime rations and almost bankrupt. The Berlin Area Plan of 1 May 1945 estimated approximately 600,000 United Nations Displaced Persons (UNDP) in Greater Berlin, of whom 400,000 were believed to be in the British and American sectors. It was also anticipated that one million refugees and co-belligerent DP might be in the two sectors. According to the Area Plan, military government authorities were to care for the UNDP, using both military personnel and the United Nations Relief and Rehabilitation Administration. Furthermore, refugees were to be the responsibility of the civilian authorities under the direct supervision of the sector Commanding General.

At the time British forces entered, the movement of DP through Berlin had decreased, principally because of the Soviets' order requiring them to leave Berlin by 1 July. An anticipated influx from the Soviet Zone of Occupation soon appeared. During the period of 8 July to 30 September, 7,325 DP were received and 6,540 were repatriated or evacuated from the British Sector. The majority of the DPs were French, Swiss, Dutch and Belgian. Evacuation was accomplished by road to the trans-loading point at Helmstedt in the British Zone of Occupation. At the beginning of the occupation, the handling of Recovered Allied Military Personnel (RAMP) was a problem of greater proportion than that of DP. However, since the majority of RAMP were nationals of Western Europe, or Italians, they were processed similarly to the DP. During the time, 2,200 RAMP, including 1,052 Italians who had fought with the Red Army after being liberated from German prisoner of war camps, were evacuated by air, road and rail to the British transit camp at Brunswick in the British zone. British nationals who for family reasons had chosen to stay in Berlin during the war were handed over to the British authorities by the Soviets, who in turn passed them on to the British Red Cross. Although the Soviets had eliminated any necessity for British troops to demobilise German armed forces in Berlin, the number of disarmed former enemy military personnel in the city, after the British entry, required some organisation by the Commanding General for their collection and evacuation. These people were an additional burden on the already inadequate local food and housing facilities. In the first month of occupation, numerous parades and ceremonies were held to herald the new era of peace.

British Military Government, Berlin Area - Entry to Berlin

**The** first British troops to enter Berlin was a reconnaissance party on 1 July 1945. A detachment of the Military Government Berlin Area, British, arrived a day later under its commander Brigadier W. Hinde. The main body reached Berlin on 4 July under the command of the first Commandant, Major General Lyne.

**Greater Berlin 12 July 1945**          **Greater Berlin 12 August 1945 - 02 October 1990**

**With** the signing of the capitulation of Germany at Karlshorst, Berlin on 8 May 1945 and in agreement with the London Protocol from 12 September 1944, the Military Government Berlin Area, British, took full control over its sector on 12 July 1945. At first the British sector comprised six municipal boroughs namely, Charlottenburg, Wilmersdorf, Spandau, Tiergarten, Wedding and Reinickendorf. The latter two boroughs, in accordance with the Four Powers Protocol from 26 July 1945, were given up to form the French sector.

British Military Government, Berlin Area - Headquarters Berlin

**The** British Military Government, established their headquarters on 4 July 1945 at Wilmersdorf town hall which became Lancaster House. An engraved plaque was unveiled by Brigadier D. de G. Broomhead and the then Mayor of Wilmersdorf, Mr. H. Dohm, on 30 April 1994 to commemorate this fact.

**Deutschlandhaus** built in 1931 at Reichskanzler-Platz, later Theodor-Heuss-Platz, was requisitioned on 4 July 1945 by the British and became British Government House. Wilmersdorf town hall and Deutschlandhaus were returned to the Berlin Senate in 1953.

British Military Government, Berlin Area - Headquarters Berlin

**The** British Military Government moved on 2 June 1953 to the complex built by Werner March for the 1936 Olympic Games on Hanns-Braun-Strasse. It remained there until its disestablishment on 2 October 1990 and the withdrawal of the Infantry Brigade in September 1994.

**After** the British Prime Minister John Major unveiled on 8 September 1994 an engraved stone in front of the Brigade's Headquarters, commemorating the fact that the buildings accommodated the British Military Government from 1953 to 1994, the Union Flag was lowered, signifying the end of the British occupation.

British Military Government, Berlin Area - Establishing control

**From** the 12 July 1945, the British Military Government were solely responsible for their sector, including providing of food and coal for the civilian population registered at the district town halls within the British sector. Signs were erected and white lines painted on pavements and roads to indicate the sector's border.

**With** the election in the western sectors in 1949 of a civilian government, the allies handed the civil administration to the new government, but retained the right to veto laws which infringed occupation rights. Inner sector border signs, except those warning of the Soviet sector and zone borders were removed.

British Military Government, Berlin Area - Prime Minister Churchill in Berlin

**With** the British Military Government in full control of its sector, Prime Minister Winston Churchill flew to Berlin and landed at Gatow airfield on 21 July 1945. Churchill was the first of the "big three", Stalin (USSR) and Truman (US), war time leaders to come to the city.

**The** hoisting of the Union Flag at the Siegessäule in Berlin, which had flown above 7 Armoured Division Headquarters at the battle of El Alamein, signified to the British troops at a full dress parade in front of Prime Minister Winston Churchill on 16 July 1945 that World War Two in Europe had finally ended.

British Military Government, Berlin Area - Fraternisation

**The** first British troops stationed in Berlin were prohibited by the British Military Government from social fraternising with Germans. In August the first step was taken to relaxed the order, by permitting soldiers to speak with children. The fraternising order for British troops was revoked on 31 October 1945

**Workable** relations with the boroughs and town halls were important for the Brigade. Annual receptions were held where the borough mayors and councillors were invited to attend. On special occasions the mayors were asked to inspect a Guard of Honour and to take the salute at the march past.

British Military Government, Berlin Area - Fraternisation

**Scarcely one knows it - when nabbed**

**With** the mass raping by Soviet troops, poor sanitation and a shortage of medicine (Penicillin), Venereal Disease (VD) had manifested in Berlin to epidemic level. In the first months of occupation, posters warning servicemen of the danger of contracting the disease were displayed in barracks, orderly rooms and mess areas.

British Military Government, Berlin Area - Black market

**From** 1945 to the currency reform on 24 June 1948 the area from the Soviet war memorial to the Brandenburg Gate was a haven for black marketers. The exchange rate was based on cigarettes such as Lucky Strike. Frequent raids and arrests by the military and the Berlin police were unable to stop the activity.

**It** had been British Government policy to pay servicemen in the currency of the country in which they were stationed. In post-war Germany it was the Mark. At the time, a soldier would be able to convert local currency into British Pounds. The problem was that the British Government was converting more Marks than it was paying out in wages. To curb British troops from dealing on the black market, and more to protect the British currency, the Ministry-of-Defence on 1 August 1946 started to pay the British Forces stationed in Berlin and in Europe in scrip currency, British Armed Forces Special Vouchers, whose purchasing powers were restricted to British military establishments. The scrip currency vouchers were withdrawn from circulation in 1979.

British Military Government, Berlin Area - Der-Berliner

**When** British Forces entered Berlin, six newspapers were appearing daily. Four of the publications were official mouthpieces of Soviet political organisations. One of the remaining two was the official organ of the Red Army and the other of the Berlin-Magistrat, the city's central governing body supervised by the Soviets. All publications were printed in the Soviet sector and were subject to pre-publication censorship from the Soviets. The first overt British newspaper, Der-Berliner appeared on 1 August. Published three times weekly and providing world wide news coverage, it soon became the most popular paper in the city. The last edition was published on 31 March 1946.

British Military Government, Berlin Area - Potsdam conference

The British Military Government provided accommodation and communications for the British delegation attending the Postdam Conference from 16 July to 2 August 1945. The delegation was first led by Prime Minister Churchill, after the 26 July general election, Prime Minister Atlee, headed the delegation.

The big three: Stalin, Truman and Churchill. With the end of World War Two, the priority of allied unity was replaced with a new challenge, the potential domination of Stalin's dictatorship in Eastern Europe. Churchill believed Stalin to be a devil-like tyrant, leading a vile system.

## Combat Arms.

**Once** the initial arrangements had been made for Four Power control of the city and the Kommandatura had its first meeting on 11 July, the British Military Government started to reduce their standing forces from 25,000 to the size of approximately one brigade. Although the title brigade was not adopted until 1953, the Order of Battle shows that as early as 1946 there were only three infantry battalions, an armoured regiment, supporting arms and service units stationed in Berlin. From 1945 to the draw-back in September 1994, British Troops Berlin were re-designated eight times.

Until the unification of Germany in 1990, the primary role of the Brigade was the defence of the city within the British sector. Other tasks included: providing guards for the Allied War Crimes Prison in Spandau, British Military Train operations, sector and wire border patrols, military policing of the British sector with the support of the civil police, maintenance of a self-contained logistic support system and provision of specialist support to the Berlin civil community such as engineers and transport. The special status of Berlin and the particular demands on the garrison were reflected in the composition and equipment of the field force: a large combat service support acknowledged the isolation of the garrison from other British military formations and the need to operate without internal or external support. Each year the combat units went to exercise at one of the major exercise areas in the British zone such as Bergen-Hohne, Soltau or Sennelager where heavy weapons could be fired and space was available for unit deployment exercises. On average a Berlin posting lasted two years.

The Brigade was always involved in the essential protocol of the military government. Guards of honour for visiting dignitaries and VIPs were a common requirement. There was also the regular commitment to major events such as the Queen's Birthday Parade, the Berlin Military Tattoo and the Allied Forces' Day Parade. The training of the Brigade concentrated on the preparedness for its operational role in defending its sector. Until the early eighties, the sight of British battle tanks and infantry deployed on the streets and in the forests were a common occurrence. With the new defence and deployment strategy for its sector, devised in 1980 by Berlin Field Force Commander, Brigadier T. N. McMicking, the garrison concentrated on urban warfare: house-to-house fighting. The need to practice the respective skills led to the construction of a Fighting City at Ruhleben training complex. Urban operations in Berlin also gave rise to a unique form of camouflage for the track-driven fighting vehicles held in Berlin.

From 1955 the funding for the occupation was financed by the West German tax payer under the Berlin Occupation Cost Budget (OCB). The budget, approximately 1,300 million DM per annum funded the running and infrastructural costs, but not the salaries and allowances of the garrison, support costs, weapons systems and warlike stores required for the defence of Berlin against external attacks. The OCB was divided between the Allies in approximate proportion to the numerical size of the respective garrisons. The West German Government financed an estimated two-thirds of the stationing costs and the Allies one third. Over 90% of the OCB was spent on goods and services in West Berlin or in West Germany.

The Berlin Stationing Agreement, signed in September 1990 by the Allies and Germany, was the document that determined how the British Forces remaining in Berlin would live and work after unification. It stated that the British (Allies) could keep up their training in and around Berlin, and that the German authorities would continue to fund the British Forces in Berlin under the Berlin Defence Cost Budget. One fundamental change with unification was that British Forces in Berlin became subject to German Law.

The shoulder sleeve insignia, nick-named by the garrison the Berlin Bomb and first worn in 1950, distinguished British troops stationed in Berlin from those in other theatres of operation. It was a black circle with a red ring, symbolising the encirclement of Berlin by the Soviet Red Army, later Berlin was added above the circle in red. In 1983, Commandant, Major General Gordon Lenniox, had the insignia removed from the uniforms. It continued to be present on documents, military vehicles and the uniform of the local recruited German Service Unit.

Combat Arms - Preparing for war

**Although** the British troops deployed and trained for conventional warfare. The Brigade planned to defend its sector by slowly luring the enemy into the city centre, where they would neutralise the supporting armour and inflict heavy casualties on the infantry, by engaging them in costly house-to house fighting.

**The** stress of exercises or deployment in the field, did not stop the average British soldiers from having a "brew up", a cup of tea.

Combat Arms - Preparing for war

# Survive to Fight

## JSP 410

**The** British trained and practised for Nuclear, Biological and Chemical (NBC) warfare. Like the Americans and French, they did not expect the Soviets or the Warsaw Pact to use Nuclear or Biological agents but did not rule out chemical non-persistent blood agents with local effect being used.

## Combat Arms - March and shoot

**The** March and Shoot Competition was a two day event aimed at testing military skills, stamina and fitness, which would be demanded in urban warfare. For fairness the competition was divided into major and minor units events with each competing team consisting of 12 soldiers and two reservists.

**Each** day, as part of the endurance and stamina tests, the teams had to complete a 20 kilometre force march with full webbing through the Grunewald Forest, crossing the Havel Lake at the widest point, approximately two kilometres, with steel hulled assault boats and a five kilometre force march back to Ruhleben.

Combat Arms - March and shoot

The degree of fitness and stamina between the competing teams were marginal. The event was won or lost in the skill at arms section of the competition. A team comprising of three or four above average firers, had a decisive advantage.

At the end of each day, after the force marches, the assault boat across of the Havel, and firing on the range, teams were confronted at Ruhleben Fighting City with an urban obstacle course which involved crawling through sewer pipes, climbing into and over buildings. The team with the least penalty points was declared the winner.

Annex C to
ORDNANCE SERVICES BERLIN
STANDING ORDERS
PART XIII - CHAPTER 1
SECTION 36

ORDERS FOR DUTY NCO

REGARDING THE USE OF THE CA TELEPHONE

(GOPSO NO 205 DATED 30 DECEMBER 1974 REFERS)

General

1. The CA telephone is to be manned 24 hours a day by the Duty Officer in the case of infantry battalions and SMUTS barracks, and by the Duty NCO in the case of 229 Sig Sqn, 247 Pro Coy and ALEXANDER Barracks.

2. Any call on the CA telephone is to be answered at once regardless of any other conversation or duty which you may be engaged on at the time.

3. The CA telephone will normally only be used for the passing of real or practice alert messages and for the daily communications test. However, in the event of an emergency and if the 309 and, where applicable the YORK exchange, telephone are out of order then the CA telephone may be used. To call the Sector Duty Officer just lift the handset off the cradle.

4. The CA telephone system is NOT secure.

Daily Communications Test

5. The daily communications tests will normally be carried out once every 24 hours. The method to be used is as follows:

   a. The Sector Duty Officer calls each of the eight units in turn by pressing the eight unit buttons followed by the 'SA' button on his control box. This will cause your telephone to ring.

   b. As soon as the Sector Duty Officer sees from his control box that all Duty Officers/NCOs have lifted their telephone handsets he will say:

   "Communications Test. Signals. Over."

   c. You will then answer as on a radio net with "OK" or whatever is applicable in the following order:

   | | |
   |---|---|
   | BROOKE Bks | "OK Out" |
   | SMUTS Bks | "OK Out" |
   | WAVELL Bks | "OK Out" |
   | MONTGOMERY Bks | "OK Out" |
   | 229 Sig Sqn | "OK Out" |
   | 247 Pro Coy RMP | "OK Out" |
   | ALEXANDER Bks | "OK Out" |
   | Alert Platoon | "OK Out" |

6. As soon as you have made your reply you will replace your handset.

Alert Messages

7. Alert messages, whether real or practice, are passed in the same way with the Sector Duty Officer calling in turn all those whom he wishes to speak to and then passing his message.

**The** aim of the Brigade call alert telephone system was to mobilize the garrison in the event of a surprise attack by Soviet or Warsaw Pact forces. A mobile alert troop from the duty battalion with supporting armour, was on permanent stand-by at the Brigade's Headquarters.

Combat Arms - Rocking Horses

The Brigade Sector Duty Officer was responsible for the call alert mobilisation. Each day during silent hours a test call was made by him to the eight garrisons Call Alert telephones which were manned 24 hours a day by either the Duty Officer or the Duty Non Commissioned Officer.

To respond to a surprise attack, the main battle tanks and armoured fighting vehicles were in a constant state of battle readiness. Call alert exercises, named Rocking Horses, were regularly held to test the garrisons response. It was expected that units would deploy to their positions within two hours of an alert call.

~~UK RESTRICTED~~

The information given in this document is not to be communicated either directly or indirectly, to the press or to any person not authorized to receive it.

# BERLIN GARRISON ROUTINE ORDERS
## BY
## BRIGADIER A MAKEPEACE-WARNE MBE
## COMMANDER BERLIN INFANTRY BRIGADE

| ISSUE NO: 43 | 09 NOVEMBER 1984 | BGRO NOS: 175 - 179 |

| BGRO NO: | | |
|---|---|---|
| | 175. | ALL ARMS COURSES - SCHOOL OF HEALTH BAOR |
| | 176. | SAMS LUXURY COACH TRAVEL |
| | 177. | FAMINE IN ETHIOPIA |
| | 178. | UNITED KINGDOM IMPORTS DEPENDANTS |
| | 179. | DRESS IN THE STADIUM NAAFI CLUB - THE SOMERSET ARMS |

GENERAL STAFF DIVISIONS G2/G3

1

~~UK RESTRICTED~~

**Berlin** Garrison Routine Orders were issued weekly on behalf of the Commander, Berlin Infantry Brigade by Headquarters Berlin Area, British. The publication informed the military in Berlin of changes in command, court marshal verdicts and disciplinary actions.

Combat Arms - Skill at arms

The annual Berlin skill at arms meeting, a three day event, gave the garrison's sharpshooters the opportunity to show their skills. It also provided units the chance to qualify for the Royal Army skill at arms meeting at Bisley, England.

For fairness, as with all the Brigade's competitive team events, the meeting was divided into: major and minor units. The team representing 14 Berlin Field Workshops REME in 1986, were winners of the minor unit's event.

Combat Arms - Women to arms

**Prior** to 5 May 1981 only service women on Provost Marshal duties were trained and issued with fire arms. With the increasing numbers of young women making a career in the armed forces the Ministry-of-Defence were compelled to review the policy on training and issuing of small arms to service women.

**The** Ministry-of-Defence directory from 5 May 1981, DGHT/10/129/AT1, stated that all service women, air, land and to sea, except medics and conscientious objectors, will be trained as in Volume 1, Infantry Training Pamphlet, Shoot to Kill, on small arms and on mobilisation or deployment be issued with such.

Combat Arms

# BERLIN BULLETIN

PUBLISHED BY EDUCATION BRANCH, HQ BERLIN INFANTRY BRIGADE

TELEPHONE: 309 43 94  FRIDAY, 12th AUGUST 1983  VOL. 34 — ISSUE No. 32

## C-in-C BAOR Visits Berlin

The new Commander-in-Chief British Army of the Rhine, General Sir Nigel Bagnall KCB CVO MC visited British Forces in Berlin on 2 and 3 August. Having visited HQ Berlin (British Sector) and BRIXMIS on 2 August, General Sir Bagnall went on to spend his second day in the City at Berlin Infantry Brigade.

*The C-in-C, the Brigade Commander and Officers watching the Heavy Ferry demonstration on the River Havel.*

*General Sir Bagnall pictured enjoying some Ranger humour with Sgt John Chusick during a FIBUA demonstration at Ruhleben Fighting City.*

*"Now I know we're on here somewhere." Lt Howard of Recce platoon briefs the C-in-C off the map.*

*The C-in-C, Brigade Commander and OC, 3 RRF discussing the Havel River crossing.*

The day began with a helicopter flight by courtesy of 7 Flt AAC. Then Brigadier A. Makepeace-Warne MBE, Commander Berlin Infantry Brigade, and the Brigade Staff gave the Commander-in-Chief an operational briefing. Next came a visit to 3 RRF exercising on the River Havel with elements of 38 (Berlin) Fd Sqn RE and 'D' Sqn QOH. The morning ended with a FIBUA demonstration by 2 R IRISH in Ruhleben Fighting City. Also on display were Brigade Headquarters 'in the field' and Ordnance Services Berlin.

The Commander-in-Chief had lunch with the Commanding Officers of Brigade units and then set off to meet a Border Patrol, The Prince of Wales's Own, at the Staaken Crossing. After a drive in 1 PWO's recce vehicles in the rain, General Bagnall inspected the new 600 m range site at Gatow and met the members of 43 Plt Sqn RE who are constructing the range.

The Commander-in-Chief then drove to RAF Gatow and boarded his aeroplane for his return flight to Rheindahlen.

A weekly periodical, the Berlin Bulletin, kept the Brigade updated with the latest garrison news and gossip. It was edited and published by Education Branch, HQ Berlin Infantry Brigade for British Forces, Berlin. The first edition appeared on 27 June 1949 and the last on 16 September 1994. The Berlin company of E. Zum was from the start responsible for the printing.

Combat Arms - Territorial Army

**The** Ministry-of-Defence extended in March 1984 their Territorial Army (TA) recruitment to Berlin. At first United Kingdom based civilians working with 38 Field Engineers RE, were recruited to form Royal Engineer PSA Berlin Pool TA. Recruitment was later extended to ex-British soldiers living in West Berlin.

**From** experience gained in other theatres of conflict and from tests, the Brigade were aware that the Warsaw Pact small arms weapons series did not have the power to penetrate double brick walls, concrete walls, breeze blocks or double rows of tightly packed wetted sandbags.

Combat Arms - London - Berlin

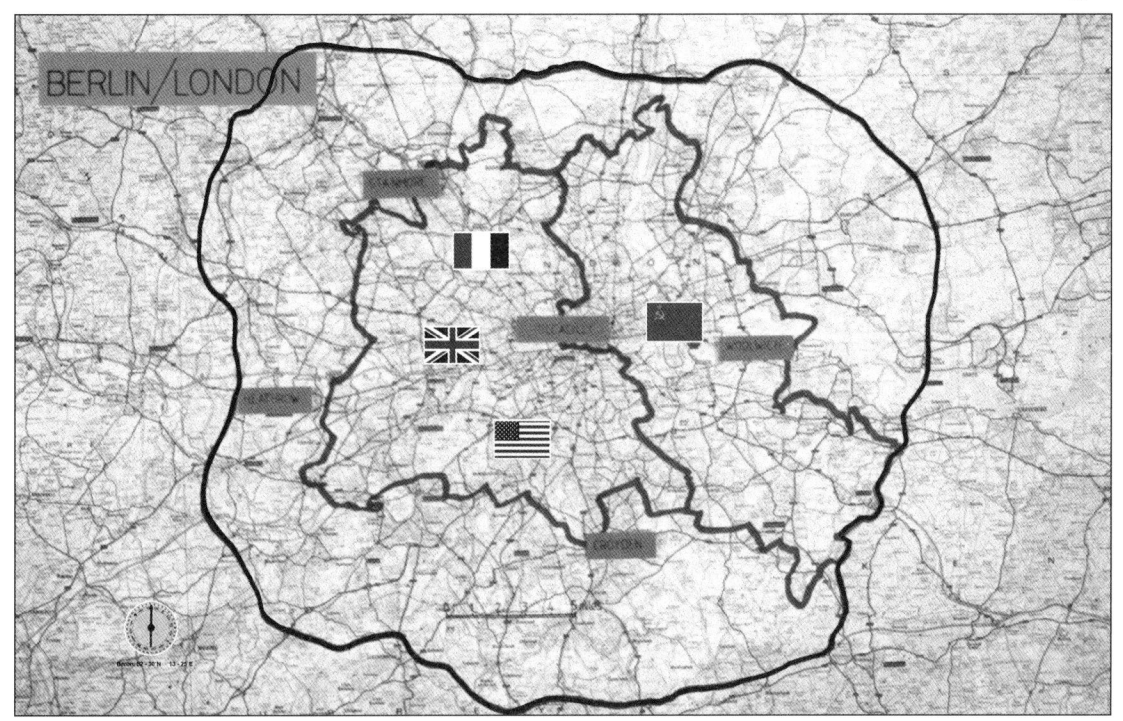

**To** show regiments and units posted to the garrison, the size of the area which had to be defended by the Allies, the Brigade gave a comparison to London. The Americans and French had similar comparisons showing New York and Paris.

**Battalions** and units newly posted to Berlin were introduced to urban warfare tactics by combat and infantry assault engineers at Ruhleben Fighting City. The training included the setting of booby traps, fortifying buildings with available materials, street craft, constructing obstacles, breaking and entering skills.

Combat Arms - Fit-to-Fight

**The** Armed Forces Memoire No. 71082, Fit-to-Fight, stated that all ranks below the age of fifty were to take and pass twice yearly the armed forces Basic and Combat Fitness Tests. Soldiers who failed the tests were reported to the physical training staff for a personal diagnostic fitness tests.

**Physical** fitness and stamina are important in urban warfare. It was not uncommon for regiments to take their Basic and Combat Fitness Tests by competing in the annual French half marathon held in the western sectors with its start and finish at the Olympic Stadium.

Combat Arms

```
                        MESSAGE FORM                    Serial No.   14 Berlin Fd Wksp 39
                                                                     F. Sigs. 266
                                                                     (Revised AUG. 81)
    LINE 1              14 BERLIN FD WKSP              CHECK BOX     (Pads of 100)
    LINE 2              1 1 APR 1986                   Routed by ....................
    LINE 3      DE      REME                           Time ........................
                                                        Perforated by................
    LINE 4
    ROUTING     Precedence-Action  Precedence-Info  DTG, Month, Year  Time ........................
    INDICATORS  ROUTINE            Routine          101000Z APR 86    For SINGLE TRANSMISSION
                                                                      Transmitted to................
                FROM    BERLIN INFBDE                                  Channel No/System ........
                TO      LIST F (LESS SRLS 2, 14, 16)                   Time ........................
                        ACTION SEEN INFO                               Operator.......................
                                                                      MESSAGE INSTRUCTIONS
                        2IC/SO ✓
                        OIC PROD
                INFO    STAFF ASST
                        ASM
                        OC                                            SECURITY CLASSIFICATION
                 30730  CSM                                           (Messages referring to a
                        TCMS                                          classified message must be
                                                                      classified RESTRICTED or
                        RAO/ST                                        above.)   NATO RESTRICTED
                        MT SGT
    GR                  CIV LAB                        SIC
                        RSO                                            YAA
```

SUBJECT CLN TERRORISM PD

ONE PD THE JSC(G) MET FOLLOWING THE BOMB ATTACK AT THE LA BELLE DISCO IN THE US SECTOR
OF WEST BERLIN IN THE EARLY HOURS OF 05 APR 86 PD

TWO PD IT WAS CONSIDERED THAT WHILST THERE WAS NO FIRM EVIDENCE AS TO RESPONSIBILITY CMM
LIBYAN INVOLVEMENT COULD NOT BE RULED OUT PD FURTHER ATTACKS OF THIS NATURE COULD WELL
OCCUR AT ANY TIME AND THESE WOULD NOT NECESSARILY BE RESTRICTED TO WEST BERLIN PD IT
APPEARS THAT AMERICANS ARE THE MAIN TARGET PD BASED ON INFORMATION CURRENTLY AVAILABLE
THE JSC(G) RECOMMENDS THAT CLN

ALFA PD WHERE UNITS ARE CO-LOCATED WITH US FORCES EXTRA VIGILANCE SHOULD BE EXERCISED PD

BRAVO PD OFF-DUTY PERSONNEL SHOULD BE ADVISED TO AVOID PLACES OF ENTERTAINMENT AND
FACILITIES KNOWN TO BE PRIMARILY USED BY US FORCES PD

THREE PD THE JSC(G) FURTHER RECOMMENDS NO CHANGE TO THE ALERT STAGE AND WILL REVIEW THE

Page 1 of 2 Pages

**The** British garrison, like the Americans and French, were aware of the threat of possible terrorist attacks from organisations such as the Irish Republican Army, Arab groups and the West German Red Army Fraction. During the Allied occupation of Berlin, bomb attacks with and without fatal injuries were directed against barracks, military personnel and Allied soft targets, such as the British Yacht Club in 1972, the French cinema Maison de France in 1983, and the American frequented discotheque La Belle in 1986.

Combat Arms - Driver training

A disused sand quarry in the Grunewald Forest, west of the Teufelsberg radar station, provided facilities for off-road driver training for track and wheeled driven vehicles.

The quarry being far from inhabited areas was not restricted to noise regulations. With the various loose surfaces, ditches, steep climbs and water graves, the quarry provided ideal conditions for off-road driver training. During the frog's breeding season the water graves and ditches were put out off bounds.

Combat Arms - More fire power

**The** garrisons fire power was increased in 1981 with the deployment of 23 combat reconnaissances vehicles, AFV 721 Fox, with a 30 mm RARDEN cannon, night vision firing capability and a 7,62 mm coax machine gun. The fast moving wheeled vehicles were ideal for supporting the infantry in urban operations.

**The** combat role of the thirteen Armoured Personal Carriers AFV 432, modified at the brigades request with the RARDEN turret, was to support the infantry in all combat zones. The eight AFV 430 were to be utilised for the transporting of munitions and if conditions permitted, the evacuation of casualties.

Combat Arms - Wall and wire patrols

**The** British patrolled their Soviet sector and zone borders from the ground and from the air. The patrols were provided by the duty battalion and coordinated by HQ Berlin Infantry Brigade. The frequency and intensity of the patrols depended on the current east-west political climate.

**Once** a month 7 Flight of the Army Air Corps, stationed at Royal Air Force Station, Gatow, had the task of photographing from the air the complete East-West Berlin sectors and Soviet zone borders. The photographic material was first analysed in Berlin before being passed on to the Ministry-of-Defence in London.

Combat Arms - Wall and wire patrols

**When** weather condition prohibited the use of vehicles, the winter outdoor adventure training in Norway came to good use. Not being renowned as being a skiing nation, West Berliners were astonished to see British troops patrolling the border on skies.

**The** Wall did not contravene the Four Powers Protocol from Potsdam. In some areas it was up to ten metres inside the Soviet sector and zone. Demonstrations directly at the western side of the Wall were outside the jurisdiction of the West Berlin police as only the military police were permitted to approach the Wall.

Combat Arms - Berlin Military Tattoo

The forerunner of the later biennial British Berlin Tattoo, was a Beating-of-Retreat, first performed in 1960 at a British trade fair in Berlin. The first Tattoo was held in 1965 at the Qlympic Stadium and grew from a one evening performance to a 12 day event with 2 shows a day.

**BRITISH BERLIN-TATTOO**

1. November 1973 um 15.00 Uhr
2. November 1973 um 15.00 und 20.00 Uhr
3. November 1973 um 15.00 und 20.00 Uhr
4. November 1973 um 14.30 und 18.30 Uhr

**DEUTSCHLANDHALLE**

To escape the weather, the event moved in 1971 from the Olympic Stadium indoors to the Deutschlandhalle on Messedamm, built by Franz Ohrtmann and Fritz Wiener and opened by Adolf Hitler on 29 November 1935. At the 1936 Berlin Qlympic Games the hall was the venue for the gymnastic and weightlifting events.

Combat Arms - Berlin Military Tattoo

**The** Tattoo's performances were divide into three parts: historical, musical, and military displays. The historical themes were taken from British and colonial history.

**At** the Tattoo music played an important role. If no bands were stationed in Berlin, bands from West Germany and Britain were invited. The Household Cavalry Mounted Band, a major attraction with the Berliners, caused considerable logistic problems for the garrison, such as the transporting and the stabling of the horses.

Combat Arms - Berlin Military Tattoo

**Before** the threats of terrorist attacks against the garrison, military display teams, who were appearing at the Tattoo, gave performances in front of the Brandenburg Gate and on the Kurfuerstendamm to promote the event and boost ticket sales.

**At** the last Tattoo, 20/23 October 1992, the Music Corps of the German Air Force were invited to participate. This was the first time in history that the military of a foreign power performed at the event.

Combat Arms - Combat Arms

**The** Brigade organised, and hosted regular army and inter-services' championships. Competitors and teams from Britain, West Germany and other theatre of operations travelled to Berlin to compete. Accommodation and messing facilities were provided by the garrison.

**Away** from the eyes of the local sport press, Hertha BSC Berlin's first division football club, was permitted by the Brigade Commander to use the training facilities at the garrison barracks. In appreciation, Hertha denoted free tickets for their home matches to the Brigade

Combat Arms - Protocol visits

**When** deployed on exercise in Berlin or at the training camps at Sennalager, Soltau or Bergen-Hohne Ranges in the British zone, the Brigade Commander visited the regiments to access the deployment and battle readiness of the Brigade's combat - arms.

**The** Commandants and Brigade Commanders, here Brigadier Alex Whitworth, MBE (October 1961 - December 1963), regularly visited the units in Berlin and the detachment at Checkpoint - Alpha (A) at Helmstedt. At these visits they were updated by the unit commanding officers on current military strength, what new equipment had arrived. During the visits they took the opportunity to meet and speak to the soldiers.

Combat Arms - Protocol visits

**Excavation** work at Alexander Barracks, Streitstrasse, Spandau in June 1977 uncovered the remains of weapons that dated back to the 19 Century. After completion of restoration work, the weapons were displayed on the walls of the all ranks social club at 14 Field Workshops in Alexander Barracks.

**The** Long Service and Good Conduct Medal is awarded to soldiers, who have successfully completed 15 years of unblemished service. Here the British Ambassador to the Federal Republic of Germany, Sir Oliver Wright adds his congratulates after conducting a medal investiture.

Combat Arms - Public relations

**Logistic** and support regiments, having long standing associations with the boroughs in the British sector, were awarded by the town halls the ancient military honour of Freedom of the Borough.

**To** commemorate the military honour, annual parades were held where units exercised their freedom rights by marching through the borough's streets with bayonets fixed, swords drawn, colours flying and drums beating.

Combat Arms - Public relations

**At** Christmas, the garrison played host to local orphanages and underprivileged children homes. During a visit to the garrison the C-in-C, BAOR, General Sir James Michael Gow, GCB deviated from the official program to attend an orphanage Christmas party in a Spandau orphanage.

**To** promote public relations with the Berlin community, the Brigade held open days. A favourite event for the Berlin children was to sit in the pilots seat of one of the three Gazelle helicopters from 7 Flight Army Air Corps stationed at RAF Gatow.

Combat Arms - Public relations

**The** British artillery in Berlin consisted of a field piece manufactured in Czechoslovakia by Skoda which had seen action in World War Two with the German Army. It was confiscated by the British in 1945 and stood gate guard at Alexander Barracks until 1994 when it was returned to the German Army.

**Because** of the strict quarantine laws on importing animals into Britain, the 1st. Battalion Royal Welsh Fusiliers, before leaving Berlin in 1994, retired the battalion's mascot goat with the rank of corporal, renowned for drinking beer and eating cigarettes, to the children's pets corner at the Berlin Zoo.

Combat Arms - Sport

**Most** popular sports were played by the Brigade, including the game of cricket, which is more associated with England than any other sporting activity. It was the secret ambition of the garrison cricketers to play for the Commandant's XI.

**A** highlight in the Berlin sporting and social calendar was the Brigade's annual polo tournament held at the 1936 Olympic polo field, the Maifeld. In 1987, the Brigade hosted the World Polo Championship. In a repeat of the 1936 Olympic Games final the American team defeated Great Britain by 5 goals to 4.

Combat Arms - Local employed labour

**From** past colonial experience the British authorities were aware that a long and successful occupation of Berlin would only be achieved with local employed civilians. In 1945, this was first restricted to catering staff, domestics, labours, cleaners and translators.

**A** squadron of the Royal Pioneer Corps, 14 Independent Pioneer and Civil Labour Unit, was responsible for the recruitment and employment of local labour. On the 2 June 1953, the unit moved from Lancaster House to Badenallee and in 1990 to the new Britannia Centre, at Wilhelmstrasse in Spandau.

Combat Arms - Local employed labour

**From** the end of 1945, the Minister-of-Defence started to reduce the armed forces from a war to a peace time force. To overcome the shortage of manpower created by the reductions, it became necessary in 1946 to start recruiting local skilled and unskilled workers such as metal workers, motor mechanics, office staff.

**German** prisoners of war released to the British sector who had the necessary skills were conscripted into the British military labour force. In the early years of the occupation, working for the military was attractive in pay and material benefits. From the fifties, recruitment of young skilled workers became difficult.

## Quadripartite control.

At the Berlin Conference (Potsdam) in Schloss-Cecilienhof (17 July - 2 August 1945) America (Truman), Britain (Churchill, then Attlee), and the USSR (Stalin) - France was not represented - agreed to divide Germany into four zones for the period of occupation. The conference did not deal especially with Berlin. Pending a peace settlement, no central German government was to be allowed, but an Allied Control Council consisting of the Commanders-in-Chief of the four armies of occupation was to exercise authority in matters affecting Germany as a whole. It was agreed that the population throughout Germany should be treated uniformly and that the country was to be considered as a single economic unit for the period of occupation. The initial members of the Control Council were Field Marshal B. Montgomery for the United Kingdom, General of the Army D. Eisenhower for the United States, Marshal G. Zhukov for the Soviet Union and General J. de Lattre-Tassigny for France.

On 30 August 1945, the Control Council Authority constituted itself and issued its first proclamation, informing the German people of the Council's existence. In the following months, the council issued a substantial number of laws, directives, and proclamations. On a number of issues the council was unable to impose its resolutions as the real power was in the hands of the Allied governments and their military governors. The political climate between the Soviets and the Western Allies quickly deteriorated, and so did their cooperation in the administration of occupied Germany. Despite Soviet protests, Britain and America pushed for economic collaboration between the zones. Over the course of 1947 and early 1948, the Western Allies started to prepare the currency reform that would introduce the Deutsche Mark. When the Soviets learnt of these plans, they claimed that these were in violation of the Berlin Agreement (Potsdam) and that the Western powers had no interest in the Control Council. On 20 March 1948, the Soviet representative, Marshal Vasily Sokolovsky, walked out of a meeting of the Control Council, never to return.

As the council could only function with the agreement of all four members, this move basically shut down the institution. The council was not formally dissolved, but ceased all activity except the operations of the Four-Power Authorities, the management of the Spandau War Crimes Prison and the Berlin Air Safety Centre. Germany, East and West, remained under military occupation in the legal sense until 15 March 1991, when the Treaty on the Final Settlement with Germany, signed on 12 September 1990 by the Foreign Ministers of the Four Powers and representatives of the West and East German governments restoring Germany's sovereignty, was ratified. The treaty officially ended the Allied Control Council and World War Two.

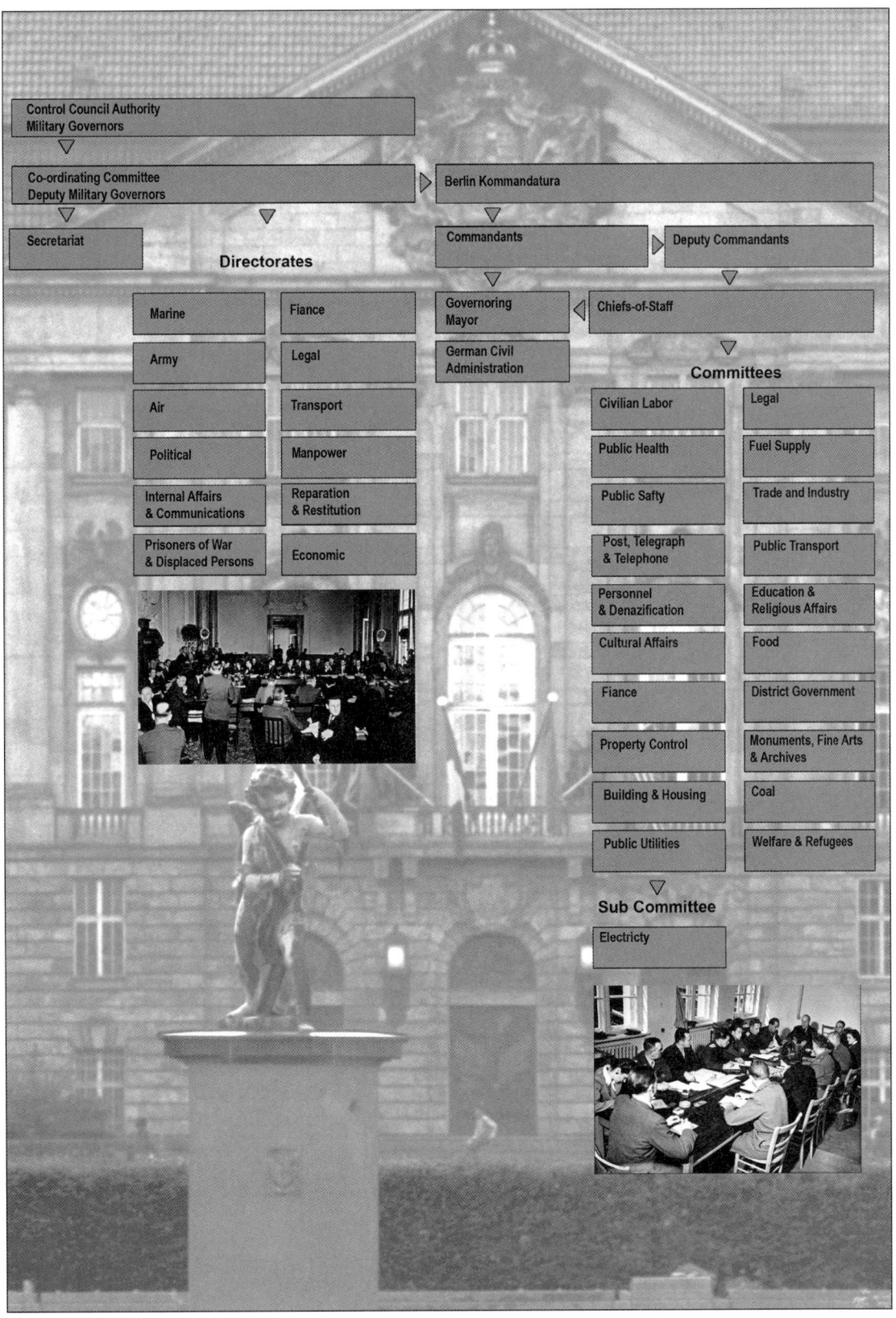

Quadripartite control - Control Council

**Control Council Authority**
Military Governors

**Co-ordinating Committee**
Deputy Military Governors

**Secretariat**

**Berlin Kommandatura**

**Commandants**

**Deputy Commandants**

**Directorates**

- Marine
- Army
- Air
- Political
- Internal Affairs & Communications
- Prisoners of War & Displaced Persons
- Fiance
- Legal
- Transport
- Manpower
- Reparation & Restitution
- Economic

**Governoring Mayor**

**German Civil Administration**

**Chiefs-of-Staff**

**Committees**

- Civilian Labor
- Public Health
- Public Safty
- Post, Telegraph & Telephone
- Personnel & Denazification
- Cultural Affairs
- Fiance
- Property Control
- Building & Housing
- Public Utilities
- Legal
- Fuel Supply
- Trade and Industry
- Public Transport
- Education & Religious Affairs
- Food
- District Government
- Monuments, Fine Arts & Archives
- Coal
- Welfare & Refugees

**Sub Committee**

- Electricty

51

Quadripartite control - Victory parades

**In** the first months of occupation endless victory parades and presentation ceremonies were held on Charlottenburger-Chaussee, named Strasse-des-17-Juni in 1953, between the Siegessäule and the Brandenburg Gate by the victorious nations.

**Prior** to taking the salute at the parade held in front of the Brandenburg Gate on 12 July 1945 in his honour, Marshal Zhukov of the Soviet army had been presented on behalf of the British Government with the Knight Grand Cross of the Honourable Order of the Bath by Field Marshal Montgomery.

Quadripartite control - Victory parades

**To** celebrate the victory over Germany. The Soviets had pasted posters of the three war time leaders throughout the city; the American President Harry Truman, the Soviet leader Joseph Stalin and Prime Minister Winston Churchill representing Great Britain and the Commonwealth.

**On** the morning of 7 September, a Quadripartite Parade was held in Berlin to commemorate the Allied victory over Japan. Four thousand infantry, 200 vehicles and four bands, representing in equal numbers the British, American, French and the Soviet Union. Marshal Zhukov, spoke briefly to the assembled troops.

Quadripartite control - Berlin Document Centre

**In** April 1945, large caches of Nazi documents intended for destruction which included 90% of the Nationalsozialistische-Deutsche-Arrbeiterpartei (NSDAP) membership lists, personnel files of the SS and documents of the German diplomatic corps's involvement in the holocaust were discovered at a paper mill near Munich. These were consolidated in Berlin under the supervision of the Allied authorities. Royal Air Force photographic technicians were posted in 1946 to the newly established Berlin Document Centre with the task of microfilming the collection. Before handing the documents over to the German Government in 1994, the Allies microfilmed the complete collection of over 52 million to assure future access for private scholars.

Quadripartite control - Berlin Document Centre

**British** prosecutors searched documents for incriminating evidence against those indicted by the International Military War Crimes Tribunal in Nuremberg. Allied denazification was not popular with German politicians. Konrad Adenauer, the first German Chancellor, passed amnesty laws neutralising the program.

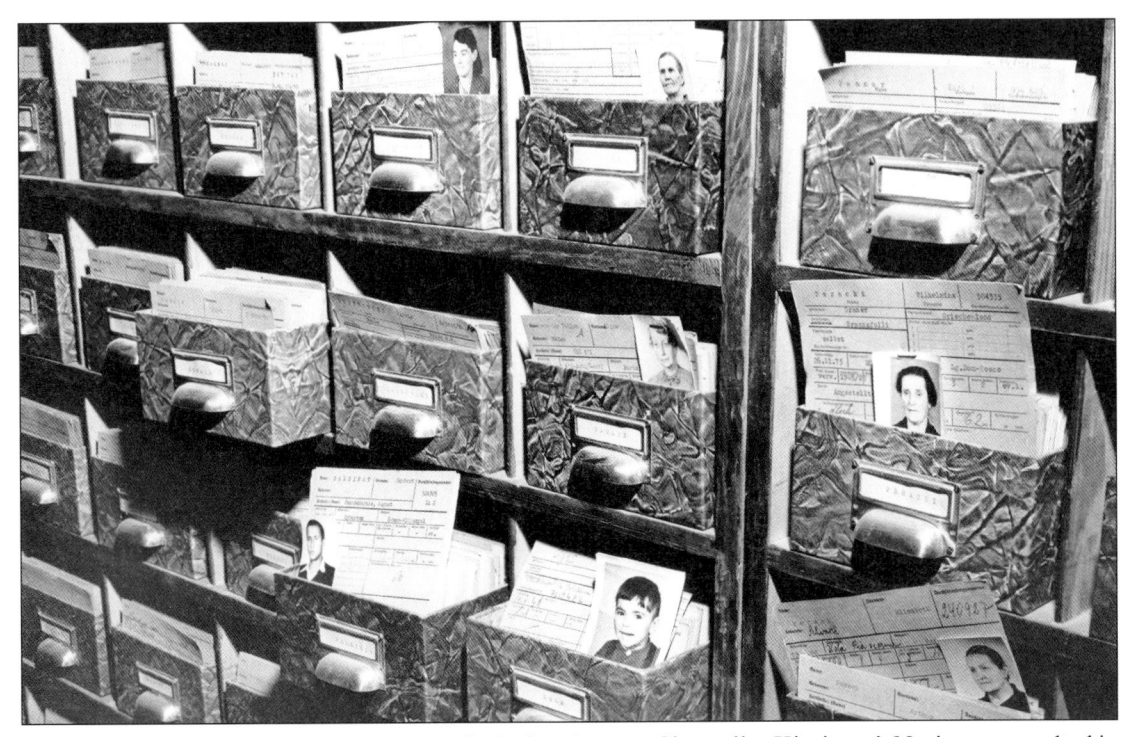

**Files** leaked to the press in March 1967, disclosing German Chancellor Kiesinger's Nazis pass, resulted in his resignation. The German Government, rife with former NSDAP members, started unsuccessful negotiations in 1968 with the Allied authorities to gain control over the document centre's collection.

Quadripartite control - Spandau prison

**The** seven convicted World War Two Nazi war criminals, sentenced to long prison terms at the International Military War Crimes Tribunal in Nuremberg in 1946, were transferred on 18 July 1947 to the 1876 built Spandau Prison on Wilhelmstrasse, to serve out their sentences.

**The** Kommandatura, including the Soviets, was responsible for the administration of the prison. The guarding of the prison rotated on a monthly schedule between the Occupational Powers, America, France, Great Britain and the Soviet Union. The financial costs were carried by the West German tax payers.

Quadripartite control - Spandau prison

**With** a protest action to highlight Rudolf Hess's, prisoner No.7, long imprisonment, a right wing extremist group, calling themselves the Free Hess Organisation, planted and detonated a explosive device at the prison on 2 October 1986 causing severe damage to the outer perimeter wall and adjacent buildings.

**The** Royal Military Police, 247 Provost Marshal Company, was responsible for the prison's outer perimeter security. The taking of photographs or loitering in the vicinity of the prison was strictly prohibited. Civilian offenders were handed over to the Berlin police.

Quadripartite control - Spandau prison

**During** an American watch, Rudolf Hess, born in Egypt, convicted in 1946 at the International Military War Crimes Tribunal in Nuremberg and since 1966 the sole inmate at Spandau prison, committed suicide on 18 August 1987 by hanging himself with an electric extension cable in his garden conservatory.

**With** Hess's death, the Allied Kommandatura ordered the prison to be immediately demolished. To stop souvenir collectors, the prison rubble was deposited in the security compound at the rear of the British live firing ranges on Potsdamer-Chaussee, Gatow.

Quadripartite control - Berlin Air Safety Centre

The Berlin Air Safety Centre (BASC) was established by the Allied Control Authority Coordinating Committee on 12 December 1945. Operations started in February 1946 under Quadripartite Flight Rules, paragraph 4 of the agreement for the air safety within the Berlin air corridors and the Berlin Control Zone.

BASC was housed in the former German appeal court's building at Kleistpark. The building is better known for Hitler's notorious Peoples Court trials which condemned among others the 20th of July 1944 plotters to death. BASC was one of two Four Powers organisations which cooperated from 1945-1990.

Quadripartite control - Berlin Air Safety Centre

**Until** its closure on 31 December 1990, the centre ensured safety of flight 24 hours a day. Each of the Four Occupying Powers was represented by a Chief Controller, a Deputy and General Duty Controller, all of which were Air Force Officers. The Soviet Controller was assisted by a Soviet interpreter.

**The** Berlin Air Route Traffic Control Centre at Tempelhof, was manned with American, British, and French air force servicemen. The centre was responsible for allied air traffic, military and civilian, flying in the three Berlin corridors and in the Berlin Control Zone. The centre remained operational until 31 December 1994.

Quadripartite control - Berlin Air Safety Centre

**An** author of an editorial in a British military journal from 1985, claimed that because of the air raids in the later months of WWII, a number of those condemned to death by Roland Freisler's court were not taken to Plötzensee for execution, but were executed by hanging from a beam in a cellar beneath Freisler's court room.

**With** a shortage of Air Traffic Controllers, the German Ministry for Air Safety (BFS) asked that the controllers at the centre continue to monitor the Berlin air space after unification. France declined the request. The German flag was added to the shield and the new Russian Federation flag replaced the Soviet flag.

## The Kommandatura.

**The** London Agreement of 12 September 1944, as amended on 30 November 1944, stipulated that an "Inter-Allied Governing Authority" (Kommandatura) would be established to direct jointly the administration of the Greater Berlin area. At the Yalta conference (4-11 February 1945) France was offered an occupation sector in Berlin.

After a flag raising ceremony at the Kommandatura building in Dahlem in the American sector on 11 July 1945, the Sector Commandants promulgated Order No.1 at their first meeting. It announced the assumption of control by the Allied Kommandatura over the city which until the 8 May had been under the authority of the Soviet Military Government. From then on, quadripartite meetings were held regularly. For the first three weeks of the Kommandatura's existence, there was no Control Council and the British Commandant remained under the full command of the Commander-in-Chief, Field Marshal Montgomery. He was left on his own to deal with an unprecedented situation in which many of the issues that were soon to split the Allies were quickly thrown up in miniature. At the beginning the Kommandatura was composed of the four Berlin Commandants each assisted by a Deputy of the four Chiefs-of-Staff and technical advisers, who staffed the quadripartite committees.

From the autumn of 1945, the conflicts between the Soviets and Western powers were sharpening in many areas, especially concerning city politics. Soviet attempts to have the communist dominated Socialist Unity Party recognised, as the only left-wing party, as it was in the Soviet zone, were resisted by the Western Allies. Although the political climate with the Soviets began to deteriorate, over 1200 agreements were still reached on a number of issues. These included the restoration of city-wide services, the establishment of a court system, common scales of rations, school reform and a procedure to allow the Commandants to remove borough officials within their own sectors.

After much difficulty, a temporary constitution was approved for the city on 13 April 1946. This provided a basis on which elections could be held. The first free elections organized in October 1946 resulted in a defeat for the communist candidates. Relations with the Soviets came to a head at a meeting of the Kommandatura on 16 June 1948 when the Soviet representative, Colonel Jelisarov, left the room stating that no further meetings would take place. During the following days Soviet representatives continued to attend some meetings of the various committees of the Allied Kommandatura until, following a declaration made by the Chief-of-Staff Colonel Kalinin on 1 July 1948, the Soviet Union ceased to participate in the Allied Kommandatura. On 13 August the Soviets emptied their offices and removed the Red Flag from the Kommandatura building on Thielallee in Zehlendorf, never to return.

Until the closing session at 0830 hours on 2 October 1990, chaired by Major General Sir Robert Corbett the Allied Kommandatura remained in law a quadripartite body, although in practice from the time of the Soviet's "walk out" only the American, British and French Commandants participated.

The Kommandatura - Kommandatura

The Kommandatura assumed full control over Greater Berlin at the first meeting on 11 July 1945 with Order No:1. As the months passed it became obvious to the western allies that the Soviet's political aims were to end the four power status and to take full control of Berlin.

At its the height, there were 20 Quadripartite committees dealing with the cities problems such as education, health. As the Soviets tried to force their political aims, committee meetings gradually developed into heated exchanges to the point that it became difficult to reach an agreement on simple technical matters.

The Kommandatura - Tripartite control

**The** Soviets, unable to achieve their political goals, decided on 16 June 1948 to take offence to the actions of Maj. Gen. Howley, USA, and walked out of the Kommandatura never to return. A week later the Soviet Chief-of-Staff announced that his delegation would no longer participate in the Quadripartite meetings.

**Following** a revision of the legal status of Berlin, the Allies decided on 12 December 1948 that the Kommandatura would continue to function as a Tripartite organisation without the fourth member and legislation passed, would only apply to the western sectors of Berlin. The last meeting was held on 2 October 1990.

The Kommandatura - Allied Staff Berlin

**The** Allied Military Committee, established on 14 September 1951, was the fore runner of the Allied Staff Berlin (ASB) which started operations on 22 January 1952. The work of the Tripartite Planning Group within the ASB was to co-operate an unified defence plan for the western sectors of Berlin against a Soviet attack.

**Until** its disestablishment by the Commandants-in-Committee, the ASB had its headquarters from June 2, 1953 to October 02, 1990, in London Block at the British Headquarters. After the re-unification of Germany on 3 October 1990, a temporary group, the Multinational Interim Co-ordinating Staff was created.

The Kommandatura - Tripartite exercises

Three Allied Tripartite exercise were held annually by the Allied Staff Berlin, the name of the exercise gave a hint to which nation was responsible for the organisation, American: Double Shuffle, British: Joint Account, French: Moulin Rouge. Soviet Flag Tours were often seen lurking in the vicinity with cameras.

**With** the planed demolition of bridges in the early stage of combat, and Berlin having numerous water ways, lakes and canals, it was essential for the defence of the city that Allied troops practise boat-skills.

The Kommandatura - Tripartite exercises

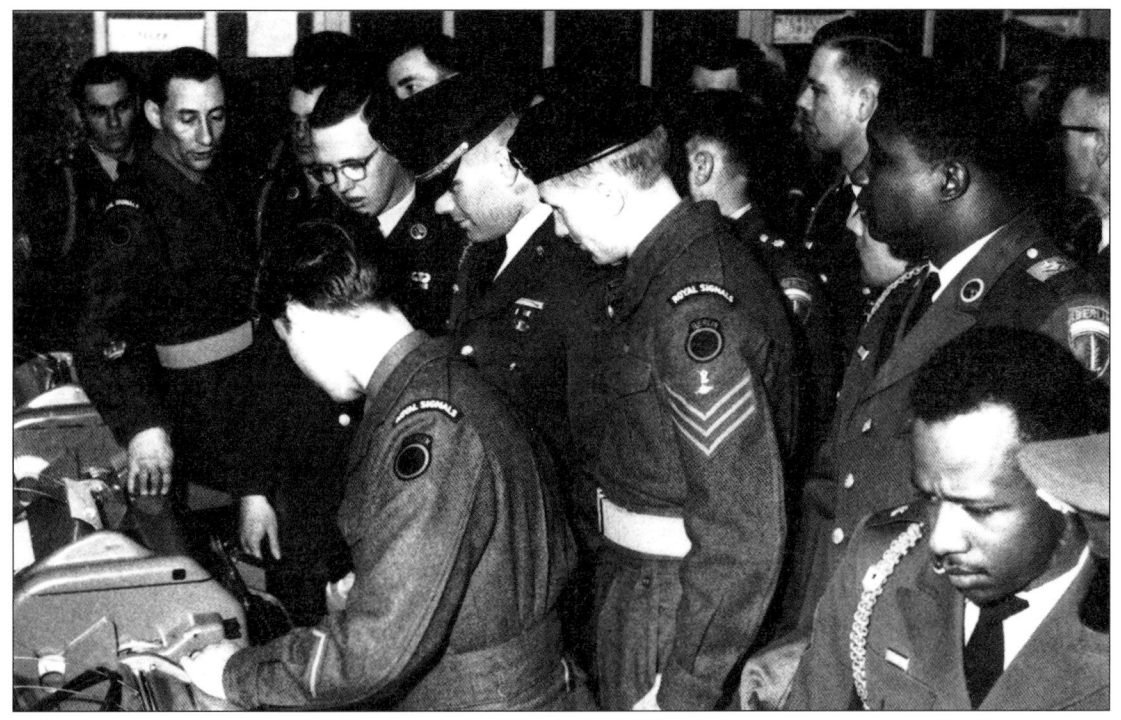

**Inter**-Allied collaboration was not confined to the exercise field, demonstrations and equipment familiarisation days were held at all levels, where Allied soldiers had the opportunity to meet their counter parts, to exchange views and learn to operate each others equipment.

**The** Chieftain Armoured Repair and Recovery Vehicle with 54,7 tons of Chobham armour, bulldozer blade, lifting boom and special capstan winch system, painted in urban camouflage and attached to the tank squadron's Light Aid Detachment raised interest with the American and French maintenance and recovery units.

ALLIED KOMMANDATURA BERLIN

BK/O(65)11
1 October, 1965

SUBJECT : Civil Defence in Berlin

TO : The Governing Mayor, Berlin

The Allied Kommandatura Berlin orders as follows:

1. Any measures that are required for protecting the civilian population of Berlin, their lives and health, dwellings, places of work and the installations and properties essential for satisfying the necessities of life against the consequences of armed attack shall be prepared and taken in Berlin.

2. The measures referred to in paragraph 1 are in particular:

   a) warning against the danger of armed attacks;

   b) institution of measures of individual protection;

   c) erection of structures both to protect the population and vital undertakings, installations and establishments;

   d) the safeguarding and preservation of cultural property;

   e) the establishment of a civil defence service for eliminating and mitigating the consequences of armed attacks.

3. Any Berlin regulations which are necessary for the implementation of this Order require express prior consent of the Allied Kommandatura before they can come into effect. They shall in principle be enacted by the Berlin Senate and promulgated in the Gesetz- und Verordnungsblatt fuer Berlin.

4. The provisions of Article II of Control Council Law No. 23 shall not prevent measures being taken under this Order and shall be considered as having been deprived of effect as regards such measures.

5. This Order shall come into force on its date of publication.

6. You are requested to acknowledge receipt of this Order, citing number and date.

FOR THE ALLIED KOMMANDATURA BERLIN

A. J. CROMBIE
Chairman Secretary

**With** the heating up in the sixties of the cold war, the Allied Commandants-in-Committee, issued on 1 October 1965 the Berlin Kommandatura Order (BKO), (65) 11, ordering the Senate to plan and introduce a Civil Defence program with the object of protecting the local population in the event of a military conflict. In 1982, the British drew up plans for the evacuation of civilians in the Brigade Combat Zone.

The Kommandatura - Civil Defence

**Under** the terms of the unconditional surrender of Germany signed at Kalshorst in May 1945, air raid shelters were classified in article 23, as instruments of war, and therefore the construction of new shelters was forbidden in Greater Berlin and the occupied zones of Germany.

**To** bypass article 23, dual-purpose underground facilities were built which would be converted into shelters in the event of a war. Within the British sector two were constructed: the subway station Siemensdamm with a bed capacity of 4,588, and the parking house on Uhland-Strasse with a bed capacity of 3,593.

The Kommandatura - Allied Forces Day Parade

The first proposal to hold a joint Allied parade was at a Commandant's-in-Meeting on 27 August 1954. The first Allied Forces Day Parade was held in April 1964 on the Strasse-des-17-Juni, thereafter it became an annual event in the Allied military calendar.

From 1968 to 1970 dissident students caused disturbances during the parades and the Berliner Morgenpost newspaper complained of the inconvenience the parade caused to motorists. As a result the Allied Commanders decided to reduce it in size and to hold it in future in front of Schloss-Charlottenburg.

The Kommandatura - Allied Forces Day Parade

**With** good public relations work and positive response from West Berliners, the Allied Commandants decided in 1976 to return the parade to the Strasse-des-17-Juni, where it remained until the last Allied Day Parade on 18 June 1989.

**Since** the beginning of the occupation, Allied/Soviet relations had been mired with threats, conflicts and walkouts. For these reasons, the Allies rejected a proposed combined farewell parade. Separate parades were held for the Allies on 18 June 1994 in West Berlin and in East Berlin for the Soviets on 31 August 1994.

The Kommandatura - Allied weapons meeting

**The** annual Allied weapons meeting, was first held in 1957. The competition first consisted of marksmen of three national teams, American, British and French, competing against each other. In 1966, the event was reorganised on a tripartite basis with each team composed of three firers from the three nations.

**Before** being permitted onto the ranges, shooters were briefed on safety and firing procedure by the Range Warden from the Brigade's training wing. Although having English and French speaking firers, no illegal discharges or accidents related to such were recorded in the events history.

## Brothers in arms, the Soviets.

**Soviet** evacuation of the British sector was not discussed until 3 July when the first elements of the 7th Armoured Division were entering Berlin. On that day a preliminary meeting of the Berlin Commandants was held, Colonel General Gorbatov, Military Commandant and Chief-of-Garrison of Greater Berlin, General Parks, General Officer Commanding United States Troops, Berlin District and Major General Lyne, General Officer Commanding British Troops, Berlin Area. At the conference General Gorbatov offered to withdraw his military personnel from the other two sectors at 2400 hours, 4 July. Major General Lyne concluded from the discussion that British Headquarters would take over complete control of the British sector at the time proposed for the Soviet evacuation by General Gorbatov. Marshal Zhukov did not support General Gorbatov's offer and on the following day sent a note to Major GeneralLyne stating that the Soviet commanders could not be withdrawn from the sector by midnight. In reply, Major General Lyne emphatically stated that civil government in the British sector was now vested solely in the British Government which he represented. On 5 July Marshal Zhukov again brought up the matter at a conference with Major General Lyne, when he said that he believed it was necessary for Soviet commanders to stay in the British sector to assure distribution of food and fuel to the civilian population and to avoid interruption of the city's routine operation, pending the adoption of uniform policies for Berlin at the first meeting of the Allied Kommandatura, then scheduled for 7 July. Major General Lyne replied that he had assumed command of the British sector in accordance with the agreement made at the 3 July meeting with General Gorbatov. He emphasized in particular that as Commanding Officer he was responsible for the sector security including the protection of critical installations. Marshal Zhukov concurred and stated that any Soviet guards remaining in the British sector would be withdrawn as soon as British guards were posted to take over their duties.

After 12 July, the only Soviet personnel on duty in the British sector with British consent were those guarding Soviet food dumps. By 27 July, the last Soviet troops had been withdrawn, making a final assertion of firmness in the maintenance of British sector security possible. Responsibility for the maintenance of law and order among British troops in Berlin and the control of their relations with the civilians and American and Soviet military personnel was discharged by the Provost Marshal. The Provost Marshal established a liaison with his peer-authorities at the Soviet, and American Headquarters and soon afterwards procedures were agreed on for the proper disposition of military personnel apprehended for misconduct in sectors other than their own. This agreement was particularly vital to the maintenance of law and order because after the removal of the initial restriction of British troops to the British sector British soldiers as well as the troops of the other nations were permitted to circulate freely throughout Greater Berlin, subject only to military curfew. The majority of the disturbances involving military personnel in the British sector concerned Soviets, or apparently Soviet troops. Because of the tendency of the Soviets to brandish weapons as a threat or as a means of intimidation, the British Commandant instructed that guards were to countenance no interference with the proper performance of their duty. A number of incidents occurred in which Soviet personnel were wounded while resisting arrest by British guards. It was the attitude of Soviet soldiers, who apparently were not discouraged by their immediate commanding officers, that as occupation troops they were entitled to all privileges of conquerors. They frequently complained that the British were treating the Germans as "allies". Soviets were known to enter German homes in groups to loot or to take over the house for a night of celebration with women found there or brought in from the streets. Various reports of such sporadic activities reached British Headquarters through appeals from German civilians or as a result of the attendant shooting or injuries. As a means of reducing the number of Soviet disturbances and in order to overcome language differences, dual British-Soviet motor patrols were established in the British sector. This practice proved very effective in the control of disorders. In addition to this step taken by the British Headquarters, the Soviets themselves undertook several measures to eliminate the number of alleged Soviet disorders in the British Sector. One of these was a 36 hour raid in the British sector by 15 Soviet patrols, for the purpose of apprehending absentees and other persons suspected of wearing Red Army uniforms without authority. Although the Soviet authority had expressed the belief on 10 August that their troops should not carry arms when off duty, and that all Commandants should issue such an order to military personnel in Berlin, the Soviets did not make such an order until early September and then limited it to Red Army personnel below commission ranks.

Brothers in arms, the Soviets - Soviet war memorial

**Located** on Charlottenburger-Chaussee, in 1953 named Strasse-des-17-Juni, is the Soviet World War II memorial. It was unveiled and dedicated on 11 November 1945 to the Soviet People's Great Patriotic War against Hitler's Germany. For the ceremony the British Guard of Honour was drawn from the 2nd. Devon Regiment.

**Three** annual wreath laying parades were and still are held by the communists at the war memorial on 21 February, Red Army and Navy Day, on 8 May to remember the cost of victory for the Soviet people over Nazi Germany in World War Two and on 11 November to celebrate the October Revolution from 1917.

Brothers in arms, the Soviets - Soviet war memorial

**With** the erection of the Berlin Wall, West Berliners held anti-Soviet demonstrations at the war memorial. To protect the Soviet guards the British cordoned the area off with barbed wire and mounted a guard post. These were made permanent with the construction of a perimeter fence and a military police guard room.

**To** strengthen the British troops guarding the war memorial and to deter future demonstrations by infuriated West Berliners, the Brigade deployed a rifle company from 1 King's Royal Rifle Corps on 17 August 1961 to the area, who encamped in front of the Reichstag.

Brothers in arms, the Soviets - Soviet war memorial

**Before** the erection of the Berlin Wall on 13 August 1961, the Soviets marched from their sector through the Brandenburg Gate to the war memorial. With the closing of the Gate, they were compelled to use the border crossing point at Friedrichstrasse and later at Invaliden-Strasse.

**At** a ceremony on 23 December 1990 the Russian Government officially handed over the war memorial for future caretaking to the Berlin Senate. In 1995 a visiting band of the Royal Gurkha Regiment were the first British troops to have a group photograph taken at the memorial.

Brothers in arms, the Soviets - Severing links

**With** the Soviets in 1952 sealing off its zone borders. The Berlin inner sector borders became a "loophole" for east block citizens wanting to vote with their feet and escape to the west. Under the pretext of visiting relations in the western sectors, an estimated three million refugees had by 1961 crossed the Soviet sector border.

**The** Soviet zone border crossing in the middle of Glienecker Bridge, was from 3 July 1953 restricted to members of the Allied Military Liaison Missions and diplomats. At the height of the Cold War the two super powers converged at the bridge on three occasions to exchange agents convicted of espionage.

Brothers in arms, the Soviets - Loophole

At the height of the workers uprising in the Soviet sector on 17 June 1953, to evade the Soviet tanks, demonstrators fled to the British sector. The Soviet's brutal suppression of the uprising, resulted in the deaths of 71 and over 6,000 demonstrators being arrested, convicted and deported to labour camps.

In a bid to stem the exodus of communist block citizens, by way of the Berlin loophole, the Soviets and East Berlin border police further tightened from 1 February 1956, access to West Berlin. Civilians and their vehicles leaving the Soviet sector were subjected to document checks.

Brothers in arms, the Soviets - Uprising , Voting with their feet

**The** Soviets, transferred the control of its border to the East Berlin civilian authorities on 20 September 1958 but, retained full control over Allied movements. Claiming that West Berlin was a haven for anti-communist activate, the East Berlin border police checked the documents of civilians entering the Soviet sector.

**To** cope with the mass exodus to the Western sectors in July and August of 1961, the Berlin Senate temporary accommodated the refugees in schools and sport halls. After registering with the Senate and screening by the Allies, the majority of the refugees were flown to reception centres in West Germany.

Brothers in arms, the Soviets - Flag tours

**The** Four Power Protocol guaranteed the occupying powers freedom of movement within the boundaries of Greater Berlin. The British demonstrated their rights with Flag Tours and site seeing trips to the Soviet sector. Attempts to visit the World War Two museum at Karlshorst were blocked by the Soviets.

**British** troops were ordered to report Soviet Flag Tour sightings in the British sector to the RMP duty desk at Brigade HQ, giving time and location of the sighting. In general, the flag tours were ignored. After August 1961, the Soviets were restricted to the Checkpoint Charlie crossing, at Friedrichstrasse.

Brothers in arms, the Soviets - Liaison with the Soviets

**Relations** with the Soviets were business-like and cordial at social events. The Soviets reacted to British protests were with counter protests, in 44 years the Soviets apologised once. Invitations to the Soviets for events such Open Days or the Queen's Birthday Parade depended on the current east-west political climate.

**With** the relaxing of the Afghan Rule in 1989, the Commander-in-Chiefs (C-in-C) of the British Army of the Rhine and Royal Air Force Germany were, after 23 years, invited on 16 September 1989 by the Soviet C-in-C, Group of Soviet Forces in Germany (GSFG) to visit his headquarters at Wuensdorf/Zossen.

## The silent dual (the intelligence war).

**From** the beginning of the occupation, an important task for the military was to assist in the field of intelligence, which was an important fact in a city deep inside the Soviet zone and surrounded by Soviet controlled military and civilian organizations.

Six British Counter Intelligence teams, one for each municipal district, began operating on 5 July 1945. Initial activities were devoted to surveying the situation and exploiting certain intelligence targets prior to the arrival of the Task Force detachment. Despite heavy damage to certain targets and the removal of others by the Soviets, some items uncovered were of particular value to the Counter Intelligence, for example the 1943 telephone directory of employees of the Reichssicherheitshauptamt (RSHA), and a list of Gestapo and "Abwehr" agents in certain occupied countries as late as 1944-45. Evidence was uncovered that the Soviets had apparently "planted" German informants in the British sector to report on British intelligence operations. One type of Soviet activity, which continued without an effective solution throughout the period, was the practice of Soviet agents making arrests in the British sector without consent of the British authorities. Some incidents of this nature occurred because certain Soviet agencies continued to maintain offices operating in the British sector after the official withdrawal of the Soviets from the British sector on 12 July.

The Roberts/Malinin Agreement from 1946 permitted a British Military Liaison Missions (BRIXMIS) to operate in the Soviet zone, while granting the Soviets the same privilege (SOXMIS) in the British zone.

In 1954-56, the British and the American secret services successfully tapped into the underground telephone network, which had been laid in 1938, connecting the Wehrmacht barracks in and around Berlin with the Communications Headquarters (HQ) at Wunsdorf/Zossen. At the end of World War Two, the Soviets occupied the Wehrmacht barracks and in 1949 redeployed the Soviet Military Administration in Germany HQ from Potsdam to the former Wehrmacht HQ at Wunsdorf/Zossen.

George Blake, a member of the British Secret Intelligence Service (SIS), who had informed the Soviet KGB of the telephone-tapping operation, was posted to Berlin in 1955 with the task of recruiting agents in the Soviet sector for the British. Being free to travel unrestricted to the Soviet sector, Blake was able to meet his KGB controller, Sergei Kondrashev, without arousing suspicions. In the fifties, the SIS operations in Berlin, with their headquarters at the Olympic Stadium consisting of a staff of over 100 agents, was the largest intelligence operation outside of Britain.

East German refugees fleeing to the Western sectors were sent to Refugee Reception Centres for registration. Here they were vetted and debriefed by officers of the British Services Security Organisation (Germany). This source of information gave the first hint that the Soviets were mining uranium ore in East Germany for their nuclear weapons program. German Prisoners of War returning to the Western sectors from the Soviet Union, especially engineers and scientists were also a source of information for the British.

The highest elevation in Berlin is the Teufelsberg, an artificial mound. The radar station perched on top of the mound was the Allies eyes and ears deep inside the Soviet zone and although situated in the British sector, it was controlled by the Americans, with the British being guests. In 1988, the head of the East German intelligence service, General Markus Wolf, succeeded in recruiting for his organization US Army Sergeant James Hall and the civilian motor mechanic Yildirin Huseyin, both employed at Teufelsberg. Hall and Huseyin were exposed as communist spies in 1989 and sentenced to long prison terms by an American court. Unknown to the East Germans, Hall was selling the same secrets to the Soviets. The station closed on 12 February 1994.

Before being employed local civilian workers were vetted by military counter intelligence. Those who failed the security check were rejected for technical reasons. Civilian workers wanting to travel to the Soviet sector or Soviet zone had to apply in advance to their unit security officer for authorisation, giving details of their visit. Those travelling to the zone or to a Warsaw Pact country were debriefed by military intelligence on their return. Civilian workers who had relations in the Soviet sector and zone were targeted by Soviet and East German intelligence. During the occupation, British Counter Intelligence were able to expose workers recruited by the East Germans or the Soviets, such as Herr Werner Muths, who had been employed as civilian deputy public relations officer at RAF Gatow.

The silent dual (the intelligence war) - British Military Liaison Mission

BRIXMIS
Shoulder sleeve insignia

Unofficial insignia

The agreement signed on 16 September 1946 by the representatives of the British and Soviet Governments, Major General A. Roberts and Colonel General M. Malinin, permitted either government to establish in the others zone of occupation of Germany a military liaison mission: the British Commanders'-in-Chief Mission to the Soviet Forces in Germany (BRIXMIS) and the Soviet Military Liaison Mission to the Commander-in-Chief, British Army of Occupation, Germany (SOXMIS).

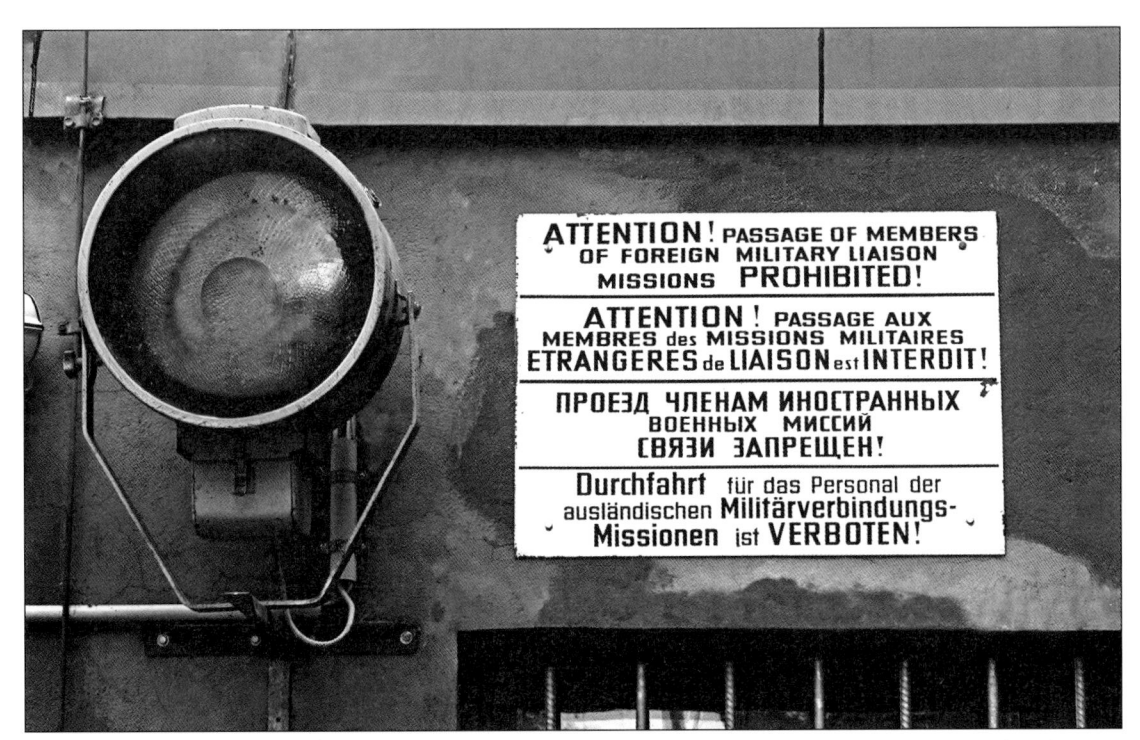

The agreement permitted each mission to have a maximum of 11 officers and 20 men, unrestricted movement, unless notified in advance of restrictions, diplomatic status, access to communications, and the right to communicate with their headquarters. The host nation were to provide provisions, fuel and accommodation.

The silent dual (the intelligence war) - British Military Liaison Mission

**The** main roles of BRIXMIS were always liaison and observation. Liaison included official visits to either lodge protests or attend functions at the Commander-in-Chief of Group of Soviet Forces in Germany Headquarters at Wuensdorf/Zossen.

**The** observation and recording role provided most of the mission's work. Tours were divided into ground and air. When on tour, which lasted from 1 to 5 days, the three-man teams, tour officer, NCO and driver, were self-sufficient and unlike the Americans and French missions, bivouac under canvas summer and winter.

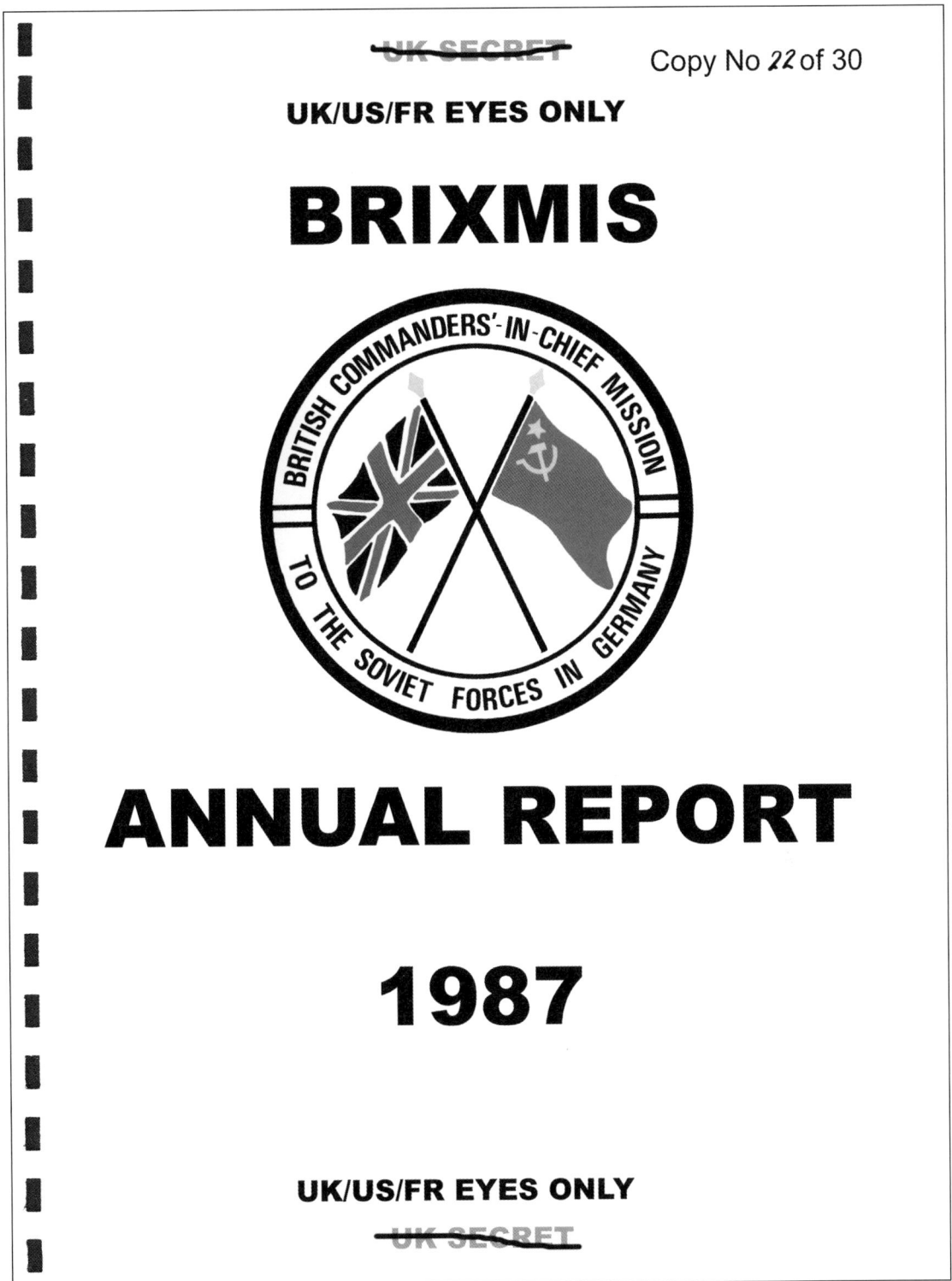

The silent dual (the intelligence war) - British Military Liaison Mission

~~UK SECRET~~

Copy No 22 of 30

**UK/US/FR EYES ONLY**

# BRIXMIS

# ANNUAL REPORT

# 1987

**UK/US/FR EYES ONLY**

~~UK SECRET~~

An UK secret classified Annual Report, limited to 30 copies, was produced by the British Military Liaison Mission (BRIXMIS). The report gave a detailed analysis of the mission's activities with comments, summaries and forecasts. Special emphasis was given to detainment and harassments by the Soviets, the East German Ministry of Interior's Secret Police (Mfs (STASI)), the National Volks Army (NVA) and the Volkspolezi (VOPO).

The silent dual (the intelligence war) - British Military Liaison Mission

**Within** the Berlin Control Zone flying radius of 20 miles were Soviet and East German barracks, training areas and government installations. The two De Havilland T10 Chipmunk two-seater aircraft stationed at RAF Gatow were from 1956 to 1990 Britain's answer to the American CIA, U2 Spy plane program.

**In** 1956 two aerial surveillance operations, Schooner and Nylon, were started which involved low flying aerial photography in the Berlin Control Zone. In the event of an emergency landing in the Soviet zone, provisions were on board to destroy the camera equipment.

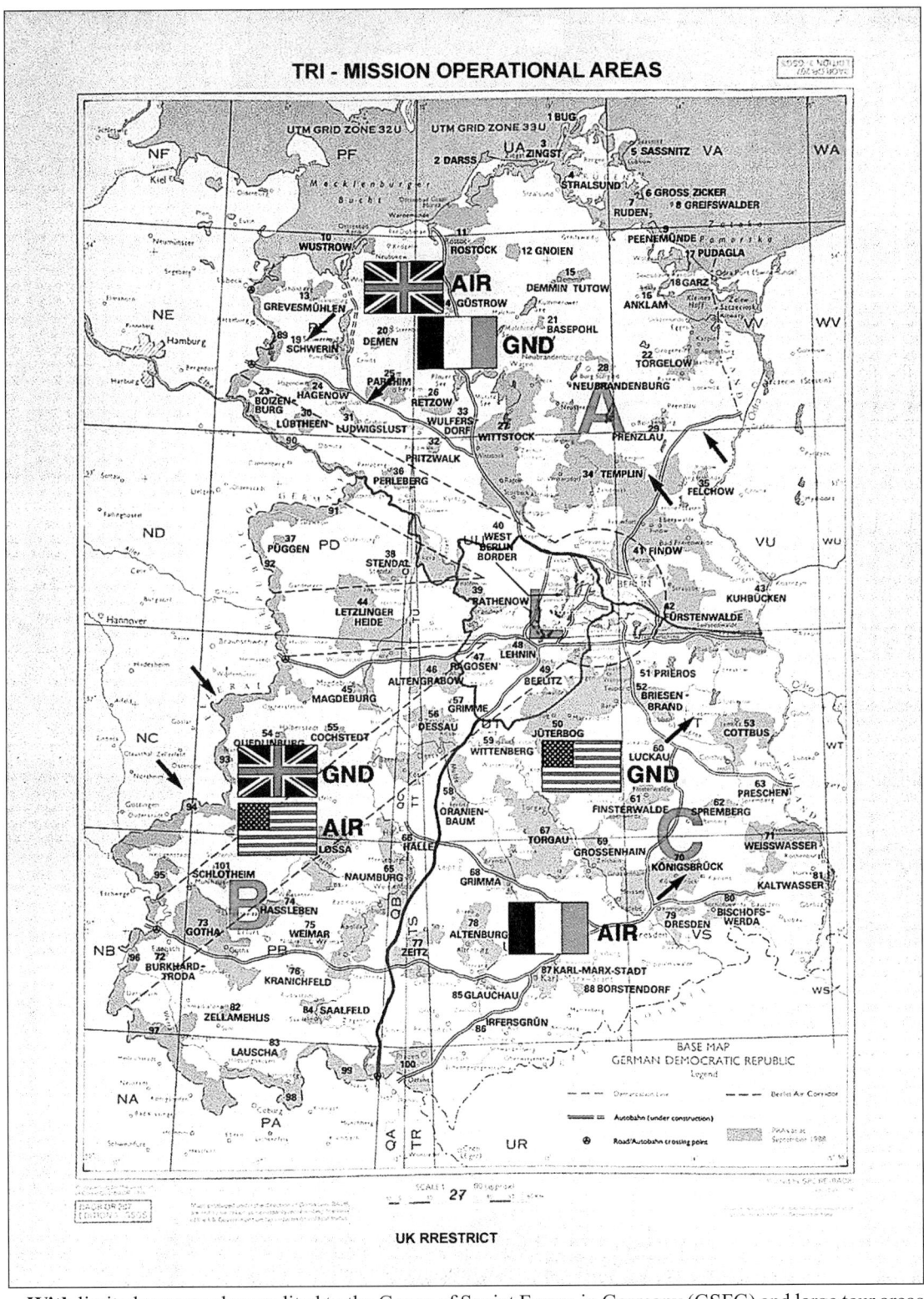

The silent dual (the intelligence war) - British Military Liaison Mission

**With** limited personnel accredited to the Group of Soviet Forces in Germany (GSFG) and large tour areas to cover. To avoid overlapping reconnaissance, the America, British and French missions divided the Soviet zone into three areas, each area was toured by a ground and an air reconnaissance team. The information gathered on the Soviets and Warsaw Pact forces was pooled.

The silent dual (the intelligence war) - British Military Liaison Mission

**Before** becoming operational, the mission's tour vehicles were put through a modification program at the Brigade's workshops which included the fitting of long range fuel tanks, off-road under body protection, additional spotlights with Infra-red capabilities, a roll over cage and most important an urination (pee) hole.

**Reconnaissance** tour teams received information of Soviet and Warsaw Pact troop and equipment movements from the Chipmunk flights, signal and intelligence units at Teufelsberg, Hangar No. 4 at RAF Gatow, Secret Intelligence Services and the Government Communications Headquarters (GCHQ) in Britain.

The silent dual (the intelligence war) - British Military Liaison Mission

**When** approaching Soviet, and East German barracks or restricted areas, tour members ran the risk of being challenged and apprehended by armed guards. Strong worded protests were delivered to the Soviets at the highest level when guards fired shots in the direction of tour members and tour vehicles.

**The** missions intelligence gathering activities were helped by the negligence and boredom of Soviet and Warsaw Pact troops, unguarded or unattended vehicles with opened doors or hatches were targeted by the tours.

The silent dual (the intelligence war) - British Military Liaison Mission

**Model** makers at 34 Base Workshops REME in England produced detailed scale models, 1/12 inch, of Soviet and Warsaw Pact vehicles and equipment from the photographs taken by the mission's ground reconnaissance tours and the Chipmunk's surveillance flights. The models were continually updated.

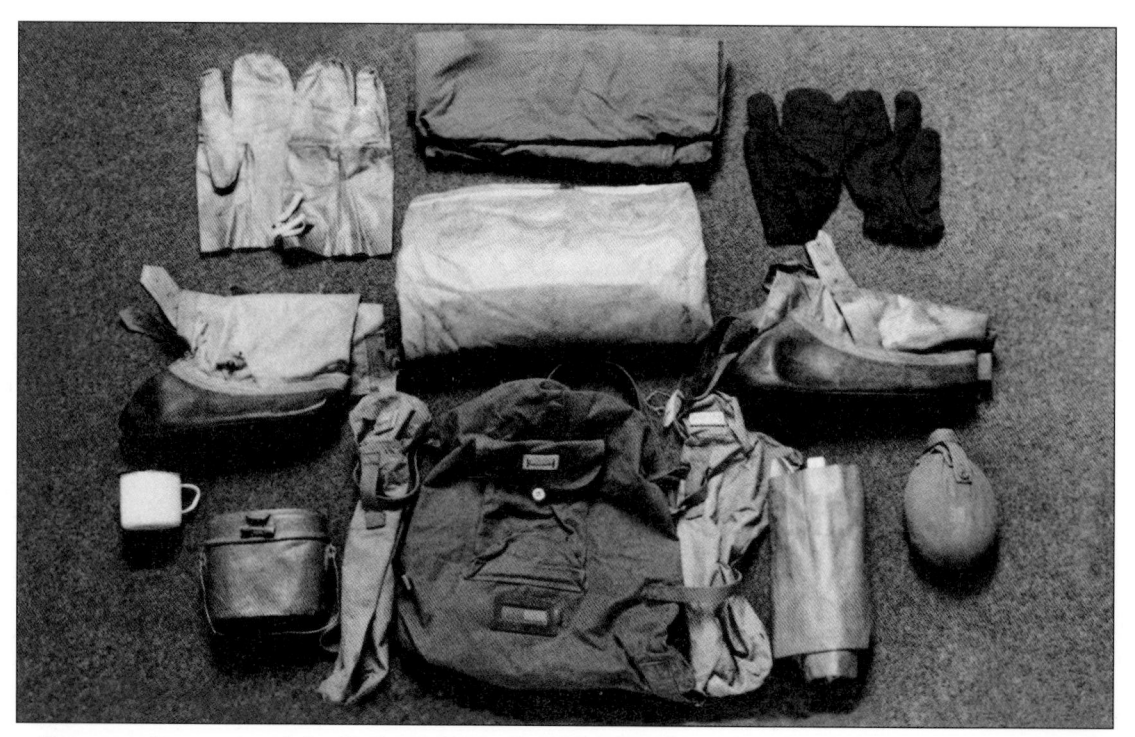

**Tour** members scourged the Soviet and East German military exercise and training areas searching for dropped or left behind equipment, such as a Soviet Nuclear, Biological and Chemical protection suit. The findings were sent to the Ministry-of-Defence in London for expert evaluation.

The silent dual (the intelligence war) - British Military Liaison Mission

> не дать ему возможности покинуть место задержания до прибытия представителей советской военной комендатуры.
> 3. Задержав автомашину с членами ИВМС, военнослужащие обязаны доложить в ближайшую от места задержания советскую военную комендатуру следующие данные: номер автомашины ИВМС; состав экипажа; время, место и причину задержания.
> Военнослужащим, задержавшим автомашину ИВМС, разрешается проверить документы у членов ее экипажа для установления их личности.
> Производить разбор обстоятельств задержания имеют право только советские военные коменданты.
> 4. Против членов миссий категорически запрещается применять силу, оружие или совершать иные действия, которые могут угрожать их безопасности. Запрещается также обыскивать членов ИВМС и их автомашины, вступать в разговоры с членами миссий и объяснять им причину задержания.
> Военнослужащие, осуществившие задержание автомашины с членами ИВМС, убывают с места задержания только с разрешения военного коменданта.
>
> Примечание: Положения настоящей Памятки не распространяются на действия часового на посту, определенные УГиКС ВС СССР.
>
> ЗНАЙ И СТРОГО ВЫПОЛНЯЙ!
> Зак. 112к.
>
> ВОИН ГСВГ, БУДЬ БДИТЕЛЕН!
> **ПАМЯТКА**
> по действиям при обнаружении и задержании автомашин с членами ИВМС
>
> Образцы номерных знаков автомашин ИВМС
>
> Автомашины Британской военной миссии связи имеют номерные знаки с 1 по 15 включительно
>
> 2 🇬🇧 БРИТАНСКАЯ ВОЕННАЯ МИССИЯ ПРИ ГСВГ
>
> Автомашины Американской военной миссии связи имеют номерные знаки с 20 по 29 включительно
>
> 22 🇺🇸 АМЕРИКАНСКАЯ ВОЕННАЯ МИССИЯ ПРИ ГСВГ
>
> Автомашины Французской военной миссии связи имеют номерные знаки с 30 по 38 включительно
>
> 32 🇫🇷 ФРАНЦУЗСКАЯ ВОЕННАЯ МИССИЯ ПРИ ГСВГ

**The** Soviet command briefed their troops stationed in East Germany on the mission's role and activities. Information cards were issued, giving instructions on reporting mission vehicles sightings, detention procedures of tour members and vehicles when confronted or ambushed in temporary and permanent restricted areas.

**Mission** member's contacts with the Soviet ranks were confined to the occasional meetings with the town patrols. Detentions of mission members or vehicles were usually made by higher ranks, such as officers and senior non-commissioned officers.

The silent dual (the intelligence war) - British Military Liaison Mission

East German Government agencies with no jurisdiction over BRIXMIS had to tolerate its activities. Harassment or provocation by the East German Ministry-of-Interior's Secret Police, named "Narks" by the Allied missions, were protested by the British mission's commander to the Soviet HQ at Wuensdorf/Zossen.

Throughout the mission's operational history, the tour members owed their successes and achievements to the Brigade's military and civilian work force, who got them into position and provided the tools to do the job. BRIXMIS ceased operations on 2 October 1990 and was disbanded on 31 December 1990.

The silent dual (the intelligence war) - Spies among us

**The** Soviet master spy Konon Molody, alias Gordon Lonsdale (insert), sentenced in 1961 to 25 years imprisonment by a British court for spying, was exchanged at Heerstrasse checkpoint, Spandau on 22 April 1964 for Greville Wynne, a British agent who had been serving an eight year sentence for espionage in a Soviet prison.

**Having** unrestricted access to West Berlin, Soviet and East German intelligence agents were able to monitor British military activities and troop strength. By scanning radio wave-lengths, British counter intelligence were able to intercept and locate communist agents transmitting from its sector.

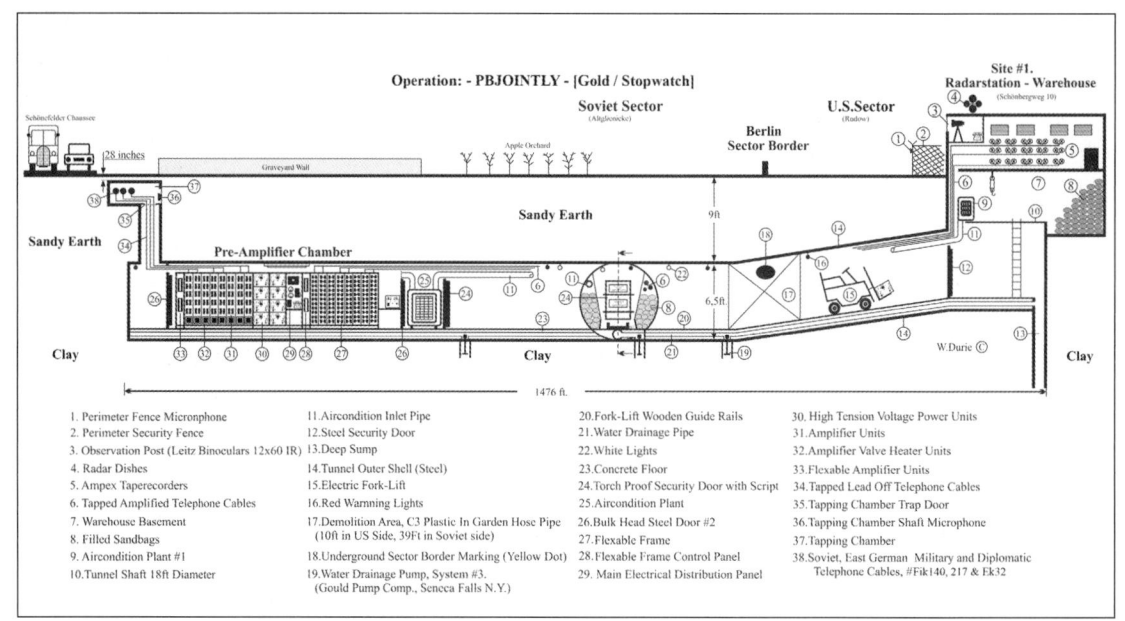

## The silent dual (the intelligence war) - Operation `PBJOINTLY`

**Operation: - PBJOINTLY - [Gold / Stopwatch]**

1. Perimeter Fence Microphone
2. Perimeter Security Fence
3. Observation Post (Leitz Binoculars 12x60 IR)
4. Radar Dishes
5. Ampex Taperecorders
6. Tapped Amplified Telephone Cables
7. Warehouse Basement
8. Filled Sandbags
9. Aircondition Plant #1
10. Tunnel Shaft 18ft Diameter
11. Aircondition Inlet Pipe
12. Steel Security Door
13. Deep Sump
14. Tunnel Outer Shell (Steel)
15. Electric Fork-Lift
16. Red Warnning Lights
17. Demolition Area, C3 Plastic In Garden Hose Pipe (10ft in US Side, 39Ft in Soviet side)
18. Underground Sector Border Marking (Yellow Dot)
19. Water Drainage Pump, System #3. (Gould Pump Comp., Seneca Falls N.Y.)
20. Fork-Lift Wooden Guide Rails
21. Water Drainage Pipe
22. White Lights
23. Concrete Floor
24. Torch Proof Security Door with Script
25. Aircondition Plant
26. Bulk Head Steel Door #2
27. Flexable Frame
28. Flexable Frame Control Panel
29. Main Electrical Distribution Panel
30. High Tension Voltage Power Units
31. Amplifier Units
32. Amplifier Valve Heater Units
33. Flexable Amplifier Units
34. Tapped Lead Off Telephone Cables
35. Tapping Chamber Trap Door
36. Tapping Chamber Shaft Microphone
37. Tapping Chamber
38. Soviet, East German Military and Diplomatic Telephone Cables, #Fik140, 217 & Ek32

**In** 1954 the British Secret Intelligence Service (SIS) and the American Central Intelligence Agency (CIA) started operation PBJOINTLY (Peter Lunn/Bill Harvey Jointly) and drove a 448 metre long tunnel at a depth of 5 metres from Rudow in the American sector and tapped into the Soviet military communications cables in the Soviet sector at Altglienicke. Unknown at the time, a member of the British Secret Service, George Blake, who took the minutes at the first SIS/CIA tunnel meeting in London on 23 December 1953, had been recruited by the Soviet Intelligence Service (KGB) during his internment in North Korea in 1951.

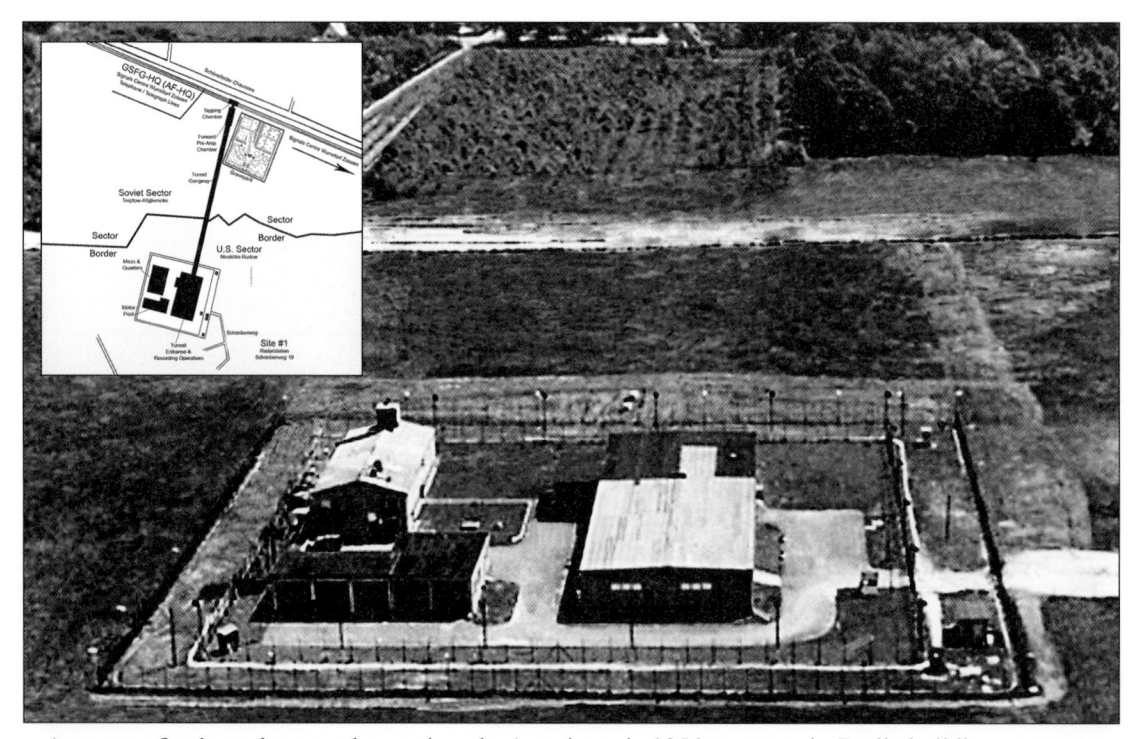

**As** a cover for the underground operation, the Americans in 1954 contracted a Berlin building company to erect three buildings at the site for the purpose of monitoring the Soviet airfield at Schoenefeld. To emphasise this, the American and British working at the site wore the uniform of the American 9539 Signal Corps.

The silent dual (the intelligence war) - Operation `PBJOINTLY´

**Men** of the United States Army Corps of Engineers started in September 1954 to drive the tunnel from the deep cellar in the main building at the radar station. A major problem encountered was the unexpected water level which at first jeopardised the tunnel's future. This was solved by the installation of water pumps.

**The** excavated earth was bagged and placed along the sides of the tunnel to stabilise it. The rest of the earth was stored in the radar station's buildings. An electric forklift, pulling rubber tired trailers, was used to transport the bagged earth and equipment along the tunnel. The digging was finalised on 25 February 1955.

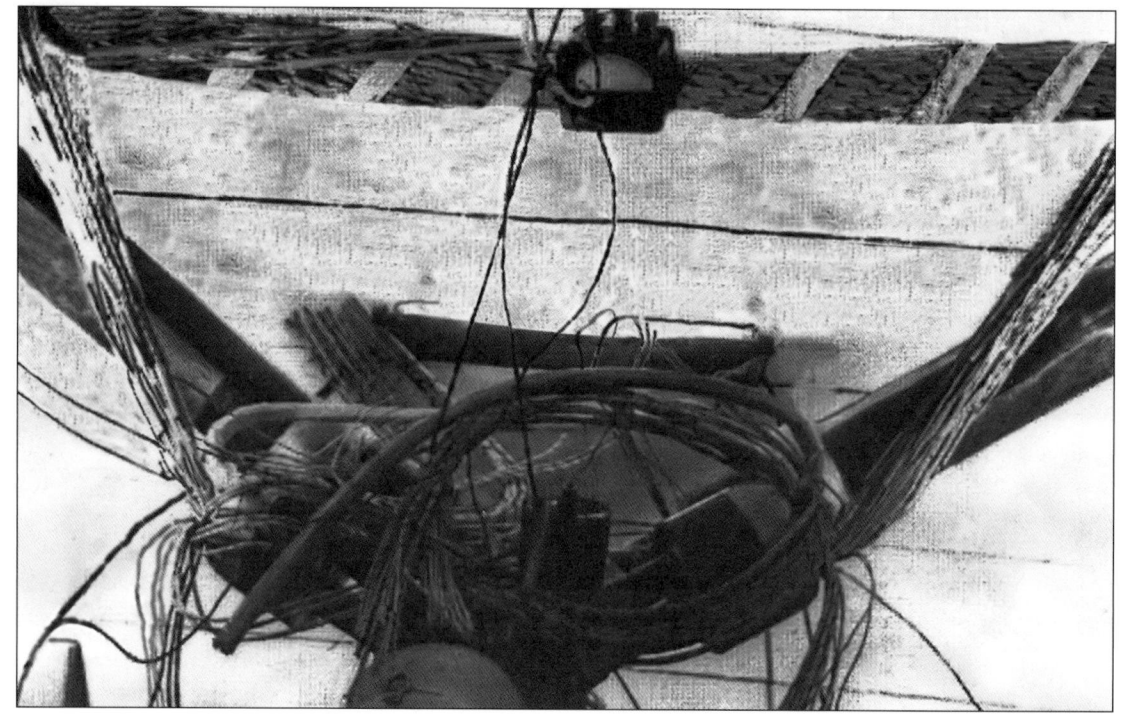

## The silent dual (the intelligence war) - Operation `PBJOINTLY´

**The** digging of the upward shaft, to expose the targeted Soviet communication cables, was undertaken by No.1 Specialist Team RE under the command of Major R. Merrell. A cable jointer from the British Communications Centre at Dollis Hill in London, Les Sparks, placed the first high impedance tap in March 1955.

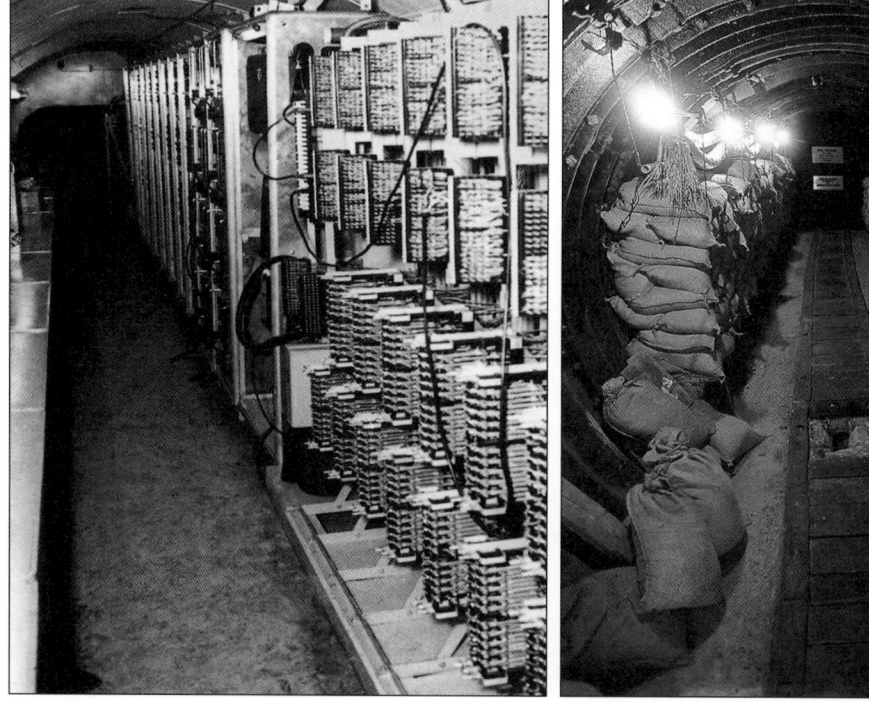

**To** strengthen the tapped signals, special amplifying equipment had been designed and developed at Dollis Hill by Blake Rymer and David Stanley's team of communications engineers who installed it in the tunnel's forward chamber. The final tap was placed on 11 May 1955.

The silent dual (the intelligence war) - Operation `PBJOINTLY´

**The** amplified telegraph and telephone signals were recorded at the radar station on banks of Amplex Model 350 double track two hour recording machines. Each night the tapes were flown to America and Britain for decrypting, translation and analysis. During its operational existence over 50,000 tape reels were recorded.

**From** the outside the compound appeared to be a conventional radar station. Nothing suggested that from the cellar of the left-hand building at Rudow, the CIA/SIS spy operation PBJOINTLY started its 448 metres journey into the Soviet sector and history. The tapping operation lasted 11 months and 11 days.

The silent dual (the intelligence war) - Operation `PBJOINTLY'

The Soviets, on the pretext of a faulty cable, exposed the operation on 22 April 1956 and blamed the Americans. The tunnel was rediscovered in May 1996 by the former army photograph William Durie. A seven metre section was successfully excavated on 22 September 1997.

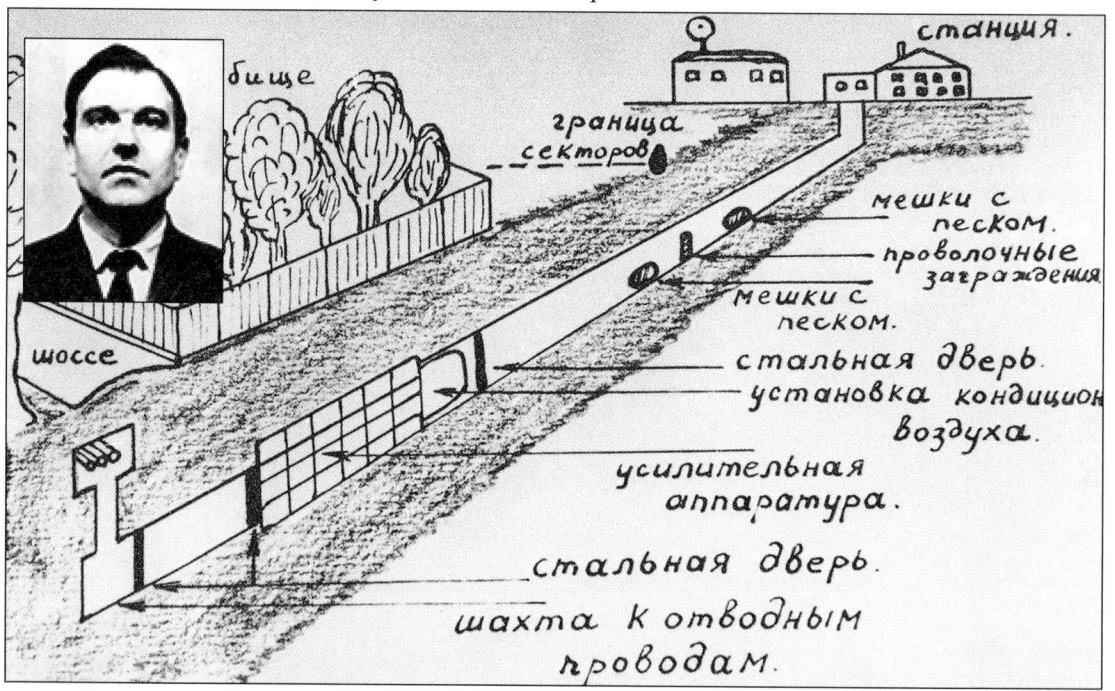

To divert CIA and SIS suspicions from a double agent. The Soviets at a press conference in East Berlin on 26 April 1956 revealed the tunnel and handed the press a sketch showing the entrance to the tunnel under the wrong building. The British were informed of Blake's KGB activities from a Polish intelligence officer, code name Sniper, who defected to the west in 1961. Blake was sentenced by a London court to 42 years imprisonment. In 1966 Blake escaped from prison and made his way to Moscow where he now still lives.

The silent dual (the intelligence war) - Spy in the sky

**An** American spy satellite orbiting at an altitude of 400 miles provided on 3 May 1965 the first satellite images of Berlin. From the photographs British military intelligence was able to locate Soviet and East German military facilities and training areas. It also outlined the route of the Berlin Wall through and around the divided city.

99

The silent dual (the intelligence war) - Fieldstation `Teufelsberg´

**The** highest elevation point in Berlin, 120 metres above sea level, is artificial. It was constructed between 1955/1957 on top of the ruins of Albert Speer's Military Technical Academy from World War Two city rubble. With the Teufelsee being near, the Berliners baptised the mound the Teufelsberg (Devil's Hill).

**American** mobile signal units were first to take advantage of the extra elevation deep inside the Soviet zone. With the man made hill being in the British sector, the Americans formally leased the site from the British and named it Site No. 4 Fieldstation Berlin. At first mobile signal units were deployed at the site.

The silent dual (the intelligence war) - Fieldstation `Teufelsberg´

**The** unexpected erection of the Berlin Wall on 13 August 1961 emphasised to the American and British intelligence communities in Berlin, the need for a modern electronic early warning surveillance system. In 1962 the mobile units stationed at Teufelsberg were gradually replaced with permanent constructions.

**In** 1962 the British Government Communication Headquarters (GCHQ) in London leased back from the Americans a part of the site and established their own signal station at the compound. British units stationed at the site were detachments from 26 Signals Squadron, RAF and from the Army's 13 Signals Regiment.

The silent dual (the intelligence war) - Fieldstation `Teufelsberg´

**The** electronic and later computerised signal surveillance and recording equipment installed at the fieldstation was state of the art. In 1981 the first transatlantic E-Mails were transmitted from the fieldstation.

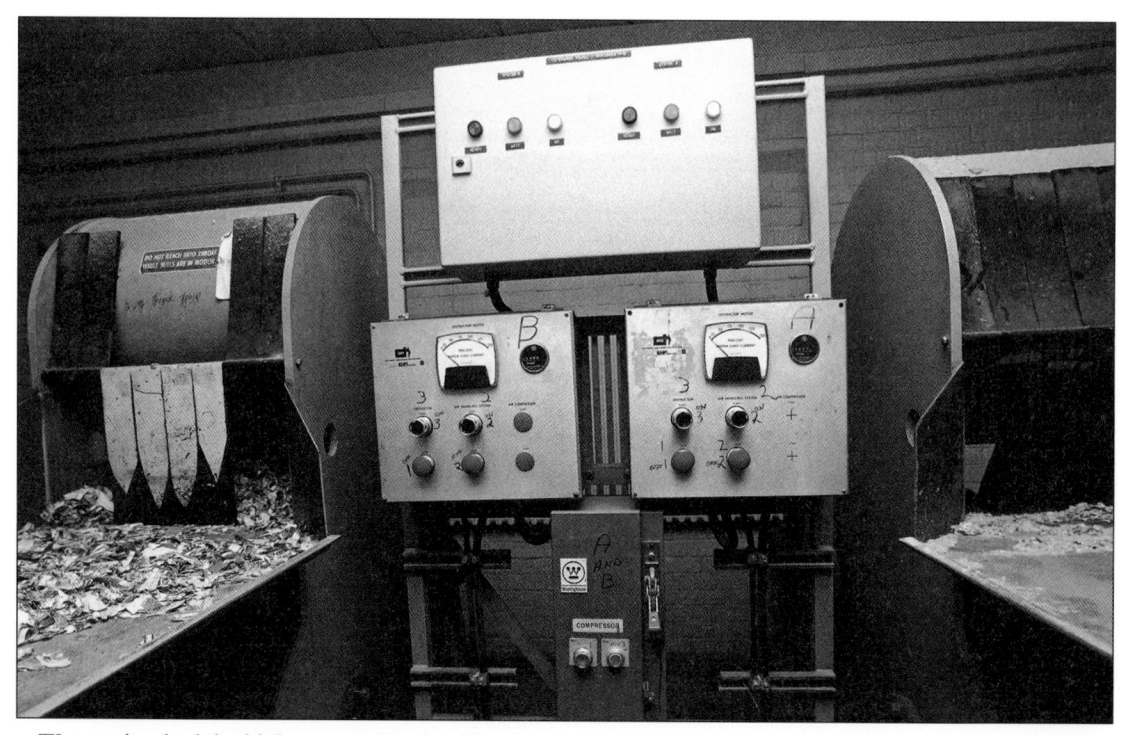

**The** station had the highest security classification in Berlin. Visitors were identified with red badges and were constantly escorted by an armed guard. Unwanted material such as documents and typewriter ribbons were shredded in crosscutting machines before being pressured burned in the stations filtered incinerators.

The silent dual (the intelligence war) - Fieldstation 'Teufelsberg'

**The** Americans and British were aware that the early warning station was high on the Soviet's list of first strike targets. They expected the Soviets would mount a heliborne attack supported by ground troops with the aim of taking the station intact. The fieldstation at Teufelsberg ceased operations on 12 February 1991.

**Hangar** No. 4 installation at RAF Gatow, was a part of the British electronic signals intelligence and early warning system. Stationed at the hangar were elements from 26 Signals Squadron RAF. In the event of war, it was expected that the Soviets would attempt to capture the hangar intact.

The silent dual (the intelligence war) - Yak - 28P incident

**A** Soviet Yak 28P, flying in the Berlin Control Zone on 6 April 1966 and having lost power on both engines crashed into Stossensee, in the British sector, killing both crew-members. Salvage work by Royal Engineer divers revealed that the ejector seats had not been armed and the pilot had a gunshot wound in his head.

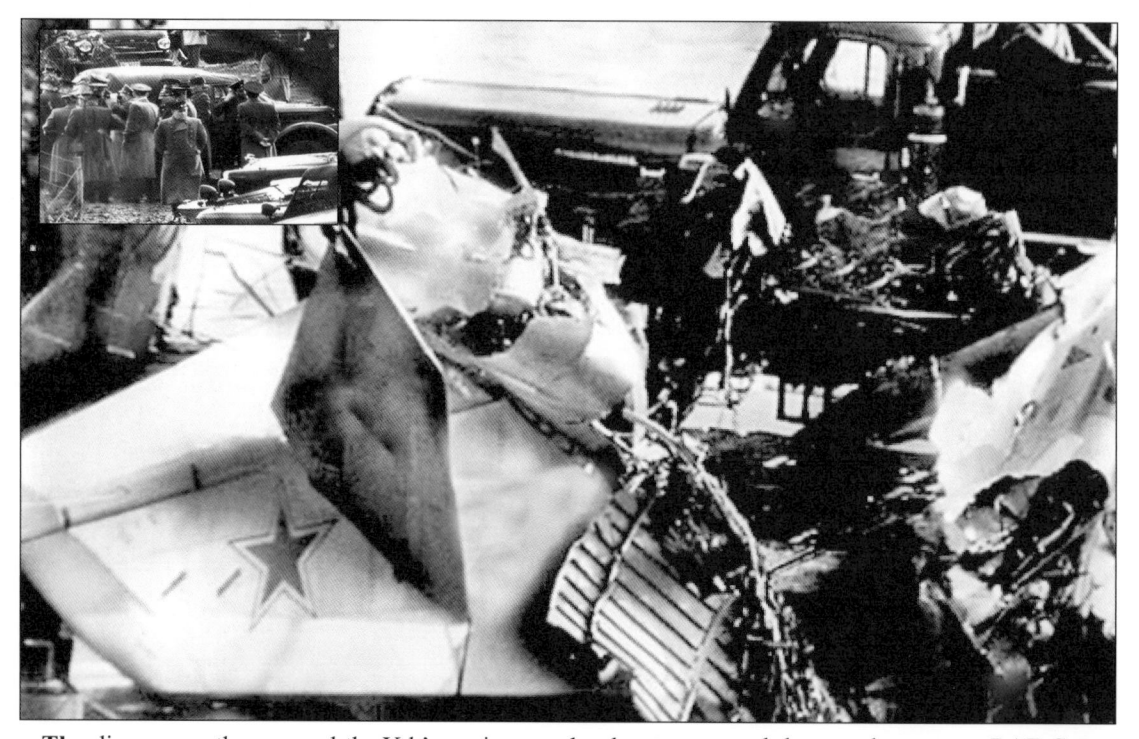

**The** divers secretly removed the Yak's engines, and radar, transported them underwater to RAF Gatow where they were flown to England for evaluation. Two days later, the engines were returned and refitted into the still submerged wreckage. The Yak was then salvaged and handed over to the Soviets.

The silent dual (the intelligence war)

To gather intelligence information on British forces in Berlin, strategic placed watch towers along the Wall and the Soviet zone border were manned with armed uniformed East German border guards equipped with 35 mm Pratika cameras fitted with 500 mm mirror lenses.

The silent dual (the intelligence war) r - East Berlin military parades

**British** uniformed observers attended the annual parades held in East Berlin. In a joint statement to the Soviets the Allied Commandants protested against the participation of East German Armed Forces, pointing out that this was a violation of the Four Powers Protocol from 1945.

**The** parades gave the British intelligence an opportunity to photograph Warsaw Pact vehicles and equipment at close range. The East German Ministry of Interior's Secret Police tried to stop photographs from being taken with blatant attempts to damage the camera equipment and harassing the observers.

## Allied access.

**In** 1945, Berlin as a quadripartite enclave one hundred and ninety-three kilometres within the Soviet Zone of Occupation presented difficult problems to the British Forces in establishing and maintaining their military supply lines. Because of Berlin's isolation from the British Zone of Occupation such lines wherever established, would have to pass through territory occupied and controlled by the armed forces of the Soviet Union. Discussions of this and similar problems of the joint occupation of Berlin had been left for the first meetings of the military commanders whose forces were to occupy Berlin.

The question of supply lines was first raised at a meeting with Marshal Zhukov on 27 June 1945. The British request of two autobahns passing through the Soviet zone was rejected by Marshal Zhukov, as he preferred one parallel motorway and rail route to be used jointly by Britain and America and suggested the Helmstedt-Magdeburg-Berlin route. Two days later at a meeting on 29 June, the Soviet Commander explained his position by stating that the number of routes desired by the British and Americans would require heavy security forces of the Red Army. This, he thought, was unnecessary since the combined British and American strength of approximately 50,000 troops should be adequately served by one motor way and one railway line. Although he did not firmly refuse the routes requested, Marshal Zhukov strongly urged acceptance of the Helmstedt-Magdeburg-Berlin route and promised that if it did not prove satisfactory, he was willing to consider other lines.

The routes proposed by the Soviet authorities, he concluded, were not to be considered an Allied corridor but had been selected because it was centrally located for both the Western Powers and permitted efficient operation in as much as Magdeburg was a junction for both road and rail lines. In order not to delay any longer the entry of British troops into Berlin, the British accepted the Soviet proposal, reserving the right to reopen negotiations at the Allied Control Council level should experience prove the facilities to be inadequate or unsatisfactory. It was further agreed that the use of the routes would be subject to such traffic and operating regulations as the Soviets might establish. It was further decided that Helmstedt, located on the autobahn west of Magdeburg at the British-Soviet border, would be the sole point of entry for British troops and supplies coming through the Soviet Zone to Berlin by road. Use of the route soon led to difficulties. The agreement with the Soviets of 29 June, which the British authorities believed would permit relatively unhampered usage of the autobahn was not so interpreted by Red Army personnel. British convoys were constantly delayed at Soviet check points and a continuous flow of supplies was maintained only by the frequent intercession of the British Commandant with the Soviet Military Administration in Germany (SMAD). In addition, a series of incidents on the autobahn during which British vehicles were stopped by Soviet troops and their occupants at gun point relieved of personal property and army supplies, made it necessary to assign armoured cars as escorts for all supply convoys. The excellent rail facilities which Berlin formerly had with the west were badly mutilated by the time the British Forces entered Berlin. The Magdeburg railway, originally a completely equipped double-track line, had been reduced to a single track without signal equipment as a result of aerial bombing and Soviet removals. Moreover, the rail bridge over the river Elbe at Magdeburg was destroyed and its reconstruction was not scheduled to be completed until 26 July. After the bridge was finished and first supply trains arrived in Berlin, frequent meetings were held with the Soviet railway officers in an attempt to improve rail traffic to and from Helmstedt. Soviet supervision of the German employees and the necessity to use British locomotives to haul both British and American trains hampered operations in general. Train schedules established by the Soviets calling for a nine-hour run from Helmstedt to Berlin proved unworkable. The average time for this one way movement as late as September was thirty-nine hours. An attempt to speed the return of empty cars to Helmstedt and Hanover by routing them on a single track line through Stendal did not alleviate the situation. Four requests by British rail officers for permission to instal military despatch offices at Magdeburg and other points along the route were refused by the Soviet. The location of any train en-route from Helmstedt was unknown until it had actually arrived in Berlin. As in the case of road traffic pilferage of supplies occurred frequently and necessitated an early increase in train guards from two to an eight-men-detail. Because of the Soviets' insistence on unilateral control of the rail line to Berlin the coordination and security essential to efficient handling of the traffic with limited facilities was lacking. These conditions continued throughout the period and prevented the scheduling of a passenger train service.

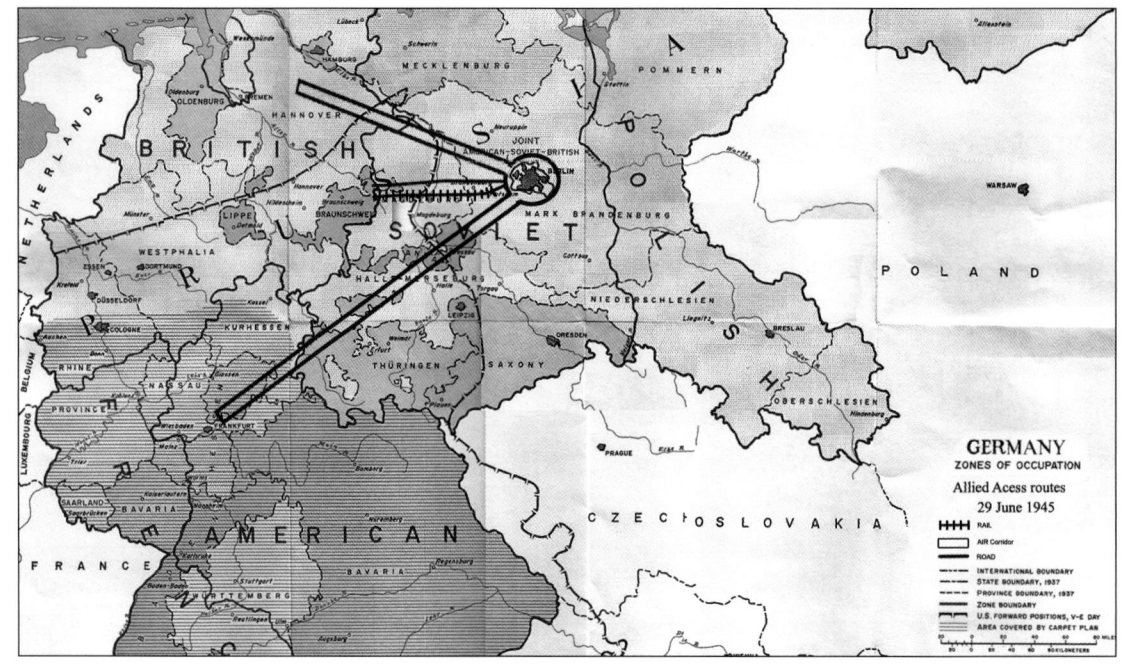

The question of Allied access to Berlin had been deferred till the end of hostilities. At a meeting on 29 June 1945, Marshal Zhukov for the Soviets informed the Allied representatives, Generals Clay (US) and Weeks (UK), that access to Berlin for the Allies would be restricted to one main highway, one rail line and two air corridors. The Air Corridor Agreement from 30 November 1945 made provision for a third air corridor.

The Berlin Control Zone with a radius of 20 miles, measured from a green painted pillar in the cellar of the Berlin Air Safety Centre (BASC) building, was part of the Quadripartite Flight Rules from 12 December 1945. The agreement made provisions for Allied pilots stationed in Berlin to book flying hours.

Allied access - Overland corridor

| | | | |
|---|---|---|---|
| | | | Form BTD/C |

**UNITED KINGDOM**
**ROYAUME UNI**
**СОЕДИНЕННОЕ КОРОЛЕВСТВО**

**MOVEMENT ORDERS**
**LAISSEZ-PASSER**
**ПУТЕВКА**

| Name<br>Nom, Prénom<br>Фамилия, Имя | Rank<br>Qualité<br>Чин | Nationality<br>Nationalité<br>Гражданство | Identity Document No.<br>Pièce d'identité No.<br>№ удостоверения личности |
|---|---|---|---|
| DURIE W. | Prof.Tech. | BRITISH | S45191105 |

is / are authorized to travel from ........ to ........ and return
est / sont autorisé(s) à se rendre de ........ à ........ et retour
уполномочен/уполномочены BERLIN в HELMSTEDT и обратно
следовать из

by train or by vehicle No.
par le train ou par voiture No.
поездом или на автомашине № ........ NP 12789 B

from (date) ........ to (date) ........ inclusive
du (date) 15 NOVEMBER 1988 au (date) 1 DECEMBER 1988 inclus
от (число) по (число) включительно

Commandant British Sector Berlin
Commandant du Secteur Britannique de Berlin
Комендантом Британского Сектора г. Берлин

Signature / Подпись: *Patrick C. Brooking*

Title / Qualité / Звание: COMMANDANT, BRITISH SECTOR BERLIN

Date / Число: 05 November 1988

**British** Military and entitled British civilians, travelling to or from Berlin by overland in a military registered vehicle or by an Allied train service required a British Travel Directory, Movement Order, which was presented to the Soviet check points for stamping, when entering and leaving the transit corridors. A Movement Order with clear Soviet markings, was a cherished Berlin trophy.

Allied access - Overland corridor

**All** Allied vehicles travelling on the overland transit corridor on route to or from Berlin had to check in or out at Allied Checkpoint Alpha at Helmstedt in the British zone. In the eighties, a compulsory 15 minute information video, outlining the thou shall nots when travelling on the corridor, was introduced.

**From** 1945 to 31 October 1969, the Allied Checkpoint Bravo (B) at the Soviet zone border was at Dreilinden. To improve border security and to cope with the increase in civilian transit traffic, the East Germans rerouted the corridor motorway in 1969 and established a new transit control terminal at Drewitz.

Allied access - Overland corridor

**With** the new corridor motorway by-passing the Allied checkpoint and the Soviets having moved their checkpoint to the new East Germany transit terminal, the Allies relocated Checkpoint Bravo to the American/Soviet zone border in the borough of Zehlendorf.

**The** British garrison was responsible for the recovery of all Allied military and military registered private vehicles stranded on the corridor between Checkpoint Bravo and kilometre-stone 98. The American detachment at Helmstedt, British zone, recovered from Checkpoint Alpha to kilometre-stone 98.

Allied access - British Military Train

The inaugural trip of the British Military Train was on 14 July 1945. The train linked the Berlin garrison with the British zone. Initially the train was a freight service pulled by a British class 4-2-8-2 freight locomotive. In August 1945, a passenger service was established which operated every day, except Christmas Day.

At first the train operated a night service from Charlottenburg Station, Berlin, to the then British Army Headquarters at Bad-Oeynhausen. Q-Movements, British Troops, were responsible for the train. The locomotives were manned by sappers and an armed guard, a corporal and six men, provided by the Brigade duty battalion.

Allied access - British Military Train

**During** the years the train's terminal in the British zone altered: first Herford, then Bielefeld followed by Hanover and finally Brunswick. Three times weekly the service operated as the Crossed Swords train to connect with the North Sea crossing, Rotterdam to Harwich in England.

**When** the BMT became a day service, it departed Berlin at 0849 hours arriving in Brunswick at 1230 hours. Before crossing into the British zone at Helmstedt, the train's documents were checked by the Soviets at Marienborn. For the return journey it departed Brunswick at 1600 hours arriving in Berlin at 1944 hours.

113

Allied access - British Military Train

The British locomotives and crews were replaced in 1949 with Deutsche Reichsbahn locomotives (East German) and crews who pulled the train from Berlin to the zone border at Marienborn. From Marienborn to the terminal at Brunswick, engines and crews from the West German Deutsche Bahn were responsible for the train.

When the train was travelling through the Soviet zone, passengers were strictly prohibited from using cameras and binoculars. Those who did not comply were severely dealt with by the Brigade Commander. Military observers who travelled daily with the train were free from such restrictions.

Allied access - British Military Train

A monthly night freight service operated from Spandau siding. It transported the armoured track and wheeled vehicles for regiments who were attending firing camps at Sennalager or Bergen-Hohne in the British zone. The service was also responsible for transporting munitions and provisions for the garrison.

Since the first passenger service in August 1945 meals were available on the military train. In the mornings on route to Brunswick breakfast was served and on the return journey to Berlin dinner by a catering staff of six. In the event of a detainment by the Soviets or East Germans the train had emergency rations for three days.

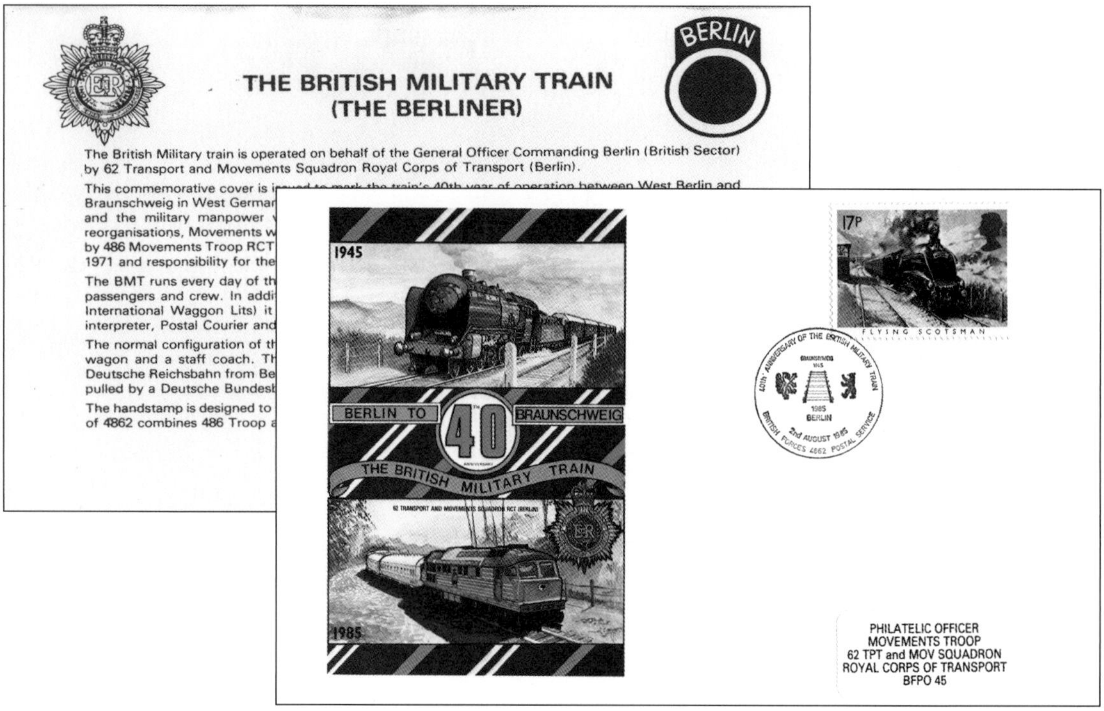

Allied access - British Military Train

**For** the Brigade's philatelist, a commemorative First Day Issue envelope was commissioned in 1985 to celebrate the British Military Train's fortieth anniversary. A postcard insert gave a brief history of the service.

**Since** 20 September 1990 the Soviet Control Office on platform No. 9 at Marienborn station had closed and with the unification of Germany there was no justification in keeping the service. The last train departed Brunswick main station at 1600 hours on 7 February 1991 destination Charlottenburg station, Berlin.

# Crisis in East Berlin.

*"Nobody intends to erect a Wall"* – Walter Ulbricht, East German President, 15 June 1961.

**Soviet** and East German obstruction of access for East Berliners to West Berlin grew during 1960 until the summer of 1961. At a conference held in Vienna in June 1961 the Soviet Union repeated its early demands (first made in 1958) for Berlin to be made a demilitarized city, while threatening to sign a separated treaty with East Germany, which itself claimed West Berlin as part of its territory. On 17 July 1961, the Western Allies rejected the Soviet demand. Meanwhile the East German state was on the verge of collapse, refugees were crossing into West Berlin at the rate of over 1,000 a day, increasing in July 1961 to over 30,000 and over 20,000 in the first 12 days of August. It became obvious to the Soviets that in order for East Germany to survive the loophole to the west had to be closed. This fact only stimulated the exit, the situation in East Germany had reached the stage where pensioners were forced to return to work in vital sectors of the economy. In July, Walter Ulbricht's government began to place restrictions on cross-border commuters. At this time about 60,000 workers were crossing daily from east to west and 7,000 in the opposite direction. On 12 August, the Warsaw Pact announced that new measures would be taken to stop "the kidnapping and human theft," that had been carried out on East German territory no reference was made of Berlin's inter-sector borders.

At 0230 hours on 13 August 1961, detachments of East German border police moved into position along the entire length of the Soviet inter-sectors borders with the west, supported by armoured vehicles, including heavy battle tanks. In 193 streets leading to West Berlin, East Berlin workers watched by border police began to dig up roads, erect barbed wire and concrete obstacles. Tram and subway links with the Western sectors were closed. The West Berlin Senate, under Willy Brandt, held a meeting on 13 August and called for Allied retaliation. Crowds of angry demonstrators, gathering on the Western side at the Brandenburg Gate, were prohibited by East German water cannons from approaching the barbed wire fence. A strong worded protest by the Allied Commandants to the Soviet Commandant, General Soloviev, on 15 August provoked further demonstrations, in which West Berliners demanded "deeds, not words" from the Allies. These demonstrations led to the belief that the Allies had failed Berlin by not taking countermeasures on and after 13 August. To demonstrate Allied determination to stand firm in Berlin, the British reinforced the Brigade with a squadron of Saracen armoured fighting vehicles and the Americans deployed an Army battle group to the city which included a number of the new M60 battle tank. The former American President and General of the Army, D. Eisenhower, commented on 22 August that the Soviet leader, Khrushchev, would merely have chuckled over the Allied reinforcements.

## Crisis in East Berlin - Closing the loophole

**To** firmly embed East Berlin (Soviet sector) in the German Democratic Republic the Soviet leader Nikita Khrushchev ordered Walter Ulbrich, the East German communist leader, to seal off access to East Berlin for West Berliners on 13 August 1961 at first with the erection of a barbed wire barrier.

**Within** days East Berlin workers replaced the barbed wire with a concrete slab wall and erected watch towers. It became apparent to the Berliners, east and west, that the division of the city was to be permanent.

Crisis in East Berlin - Checkpoint Charlie (C)

The division of Berlin with the Wall reduced Allied access to the Soviet sector, guaranteed in the Potsdam Protocol from 1945, to the American Checkpoint Charlie (C), on Friedrichstrasse. In September 1962 the checkpoint barrack was extended to accommodate elements of British and French military police.

The allies refusal to acknowledge or submit to East Berlin pass controls was a constant reminder to the communist authorities of the Four Power status of the city. The East Government with the backing of Moscow, attempted to exert its authority on the Allies by occasionally closing the Friedrichstrasse crossing.

Crisis in East Berlin - Living with the Wall

**East** Berlin's communist government, strived to create an escape proof frontier. Buildings, and property which bordered or were in the vicinity of the western sector borders were confiscated, emptied of inhabitants and demolished to create a wide no mans land. The frontier was improved with each new escape.

**After** the erection of the Wall, the majority of escape attempts either ended with the escapees being caught or shot by the East German border guards, who had orders to shoot to kill. Border guards who enforced the shooting order were rewarded with extra leave and proclaimed a Hero of the Workers State.

Crisis in East Berlin - Living with the Wall

**The** Ministry-of-Defence encouraged mayors and members of parliament to visit regiments stationed in Berlin who recruited in their constituencies. During such a visit to Berlin, the Lord Mayor-of-London, Sir Ralph Perring took special interest in how the city coped with its refuse collecting.

**The** most popular location for regimental photographs was in front of the Brandenburg Gate on the Strasse-des-17-Juni. With the Berlin Wall and the East Berlin television tower, weather permitting, in the background.

Crisis in East Berlin - Wall encounters

**Incidents** which occurred at the British/Soviet sector and zone borders were investigated by the military police. In each instance the military police refused to enter into negotiations with the East German police or border guards and demanded the Soviet Commandant be summoned as negotiation partner.

**As** a result of a partial successful escape attempt in April 1989 by three young Berliners swimming across the river Spree behind the Reichstag, the British Commandant Maj. Gen. R. Corbett ordered the combat engineers to instal scaling ropes and ladders to assist future escapees to climb the high river embankment.

## Defending its sector, "nowhere to go. . . . ".

**The** Berlin Infantry Brigade had the operational task, unique in the British Army, of defending part of a major city and therefore required its own tactical concept as a basis for realistic training and sensible planning. Before 1980 the Brigade`s Combat Zone, and defence planning for its sector was concentrated around the Brigade Administration Area at the Olympic Stadium.

As very little had been published on tactical doctrine for urban warfare, the then Berlin Brigade Commander, Brigadier T. N. McMicking, invited in December 1979 a cross section from various theatres of operations of the British military to a three day symposium in Berlin with the purpose of developing a concept based on a brigade-sized formation similar to that in Berlin for the defence of a part or a whole major European city or town. A result of the study the Berlin Fighting In Built Up-Area (FIBUA) Report was published in June 1980, which set out a detailed concept for the defence of a city, a town or a sector of Berlin. The report took into consideration the tactical doctrine of Soviet and Warsaw Pact military thinking which maintained that in any future war in Europe, FIBUA will be inevitable, together with experience gained in Northern Ireland and historical lessons learnt. Consequently a number of battles were studied from 1940 onwards, with particular emphasis on those most closely relating to the urban environment of Berlin. The study looked at the need to defend a city or town regarding its strategic position or in the case of Berlin the prospect of having nowhere to go. In order to test the 1980 FIBUA concept a series of exercises were held within West Berlin in March 1981, using derelict buildings, underground railways under construction, and tunnels at company, battalion and at Field Force level, in relation to the actual ground that was to be defended.

While many of the ideas put forward in the 1980 report were clearly well suited for Berlin, a number of problems were encountered when actually fitting infantry battalions to their allotted area of operations. The main difficulties were concerned mostly with the concept of the defensive bastion, which appeared to have a number of anomalies. Unlike the 1980 report, which had made no mention of training, the revised report published in May 1982 concentrated on the low level `nitty-gritty´ role of platoon and section commanders, who often were untrained in FIBUA until they came to Berlin. An aspect which came through strongly was the dependence on junior non-commissioned officers (JNCO) in FIBUA. It recommended that skills usually confined to Combat Engineers (Sappers) and Assault Pioneers should be taught to all infantry soldiers. The report emphasized the need to develop a package system so that new battalions posted to Berlin quickly mastered the FIBUA role. The final part of the report dealt with the suitability of the weapon systems and equipment in a FIBUA context and suggested improvements to them before the end of the century. Two points were stressed. First, finance, or rather the lack of it, was likely to continue to blunt the Brigade's ability to arm its self as it would like. Second, fighting in a built-up area would demand an extremely high standard of fitness: the difficulties of fighting from building to building, crawling through mouse holes or sewers, with added demands of additional quantities of ammunition, dictated the carriage of minimum equipment commensurate with the task in hand. Trials had established the merits of reducing webbing equipment, with a rucksack which could be dumped in section or platoon positions.

The report, Logistics In Built Up-Area (LIBUA), published the same year, looked in depth at the role of logistics especially re-supply and forward dumping to task. Recommendations for procedures which were more suitable to FIBUA were outlined.

In a paper from Major N. Holland, the OC of the Brigade's workshops, battle damage 1st and 2nd line repairs procedures were updated in order to fit into FIBUA. The major recommended that recovery teams were to be poised well forward to minimise the time between locating and recovery. The report added that time should be invested in radio operating training which was up to then seen by the workshops as a part-time occupation. Having limited manpower at his disposal, the major put forward a proposal that a Territorial Unit recruited from British civilians employed at the workshops or living in Berlin, of whom a large number were ex-service men, should be investigated by the MOD.

Foot note:

In the first Chechen/Russian War, 1994-96 the defenders of Grozny, the capital of Chechenia, based their tactics on the Brigade`s revised FIBUA report published in May 1982. The high casualties inflicted by the small defence force in the Russian attempt to capture the city forced the aggressors to withdraw.

Defending its sector, "nowhere to go . . . ."

## Ruhleben Training Complex 1981.
(Fighting City)

The training complex at Ruhleben constructed in 1981 resembled a inner city environment. To aid and analyse training, a video recording system with night vision capabilities was installed in 1986. The mock up city provided above and below ground training facilities such as multi-storey buildings, a petrol station, sewage pipes and a subway station. Soldiers stationed in Berlin referred to the Ruhleben complex as Fighting City. After the British withdrawal, the training facility was taken over by the Berlin police.

*"He who fights and moves judiciously away lives to fight another Day".*
(Anon)

Defending its sector, "nowhere to go . . . ." - Fighting in Built up Area

~~UK RESTRICTED~~

| SEEN | INIT |
|---|---|
| OC | |
| WKSP OFFR | |
| TSO | |
| OIC MAN SVCS | |
| STAFF ASST | |
| ASM | |
| OC | |
| CSM | |

# THE BERLIN FIBUA REPORT

## JUNE 1980

~~UK RESTRICTED~~

*Defending its sector, "nowhere to go . . . ." - Fighting in Built up Area*

ANNEX B TO
PART 1 SECTION B
BERLIN FIBUA REPORT
DATED    JUN 80

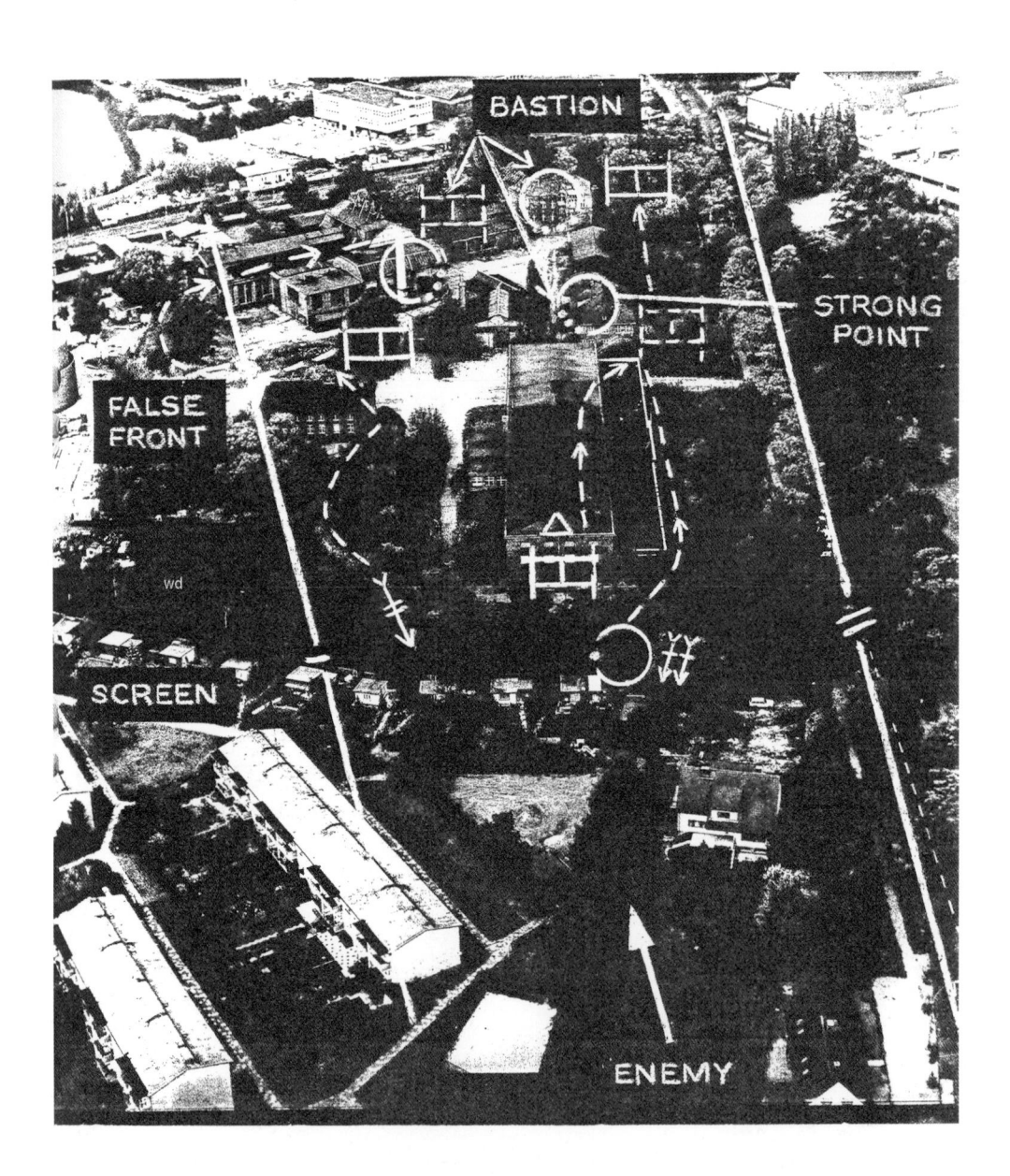

~~UK SECRET~~
UK/AUS/CAN/US EYES ONLY

BASTION

STRONG POINT

FALSE FRONT

wd

SCREEN

ENEMY

~~UK SECRET~~
UK/AUS/CAN/US EYES ONLY
1B - B - 1

The report from June 1980 recommended that the defence of a city like Berlin with limited ground troops and armour, with no reinforcement from outside or local support, and no where to go, would be more effective and costly to the attackers if the Brigade Combat Zone (BCZ) was divided into three, Obstacle zone (OZ), Delay zone (DZ) and Final defence zone (FDZ).

Defending its sector, "nowhere to go . . . ." - Obstacle zone, `shoot and scoot´

**When** it came to engagement, a covering guard force in front of the OZ was to maintain constant contact with the enemy to prevent surprise and identify main enemy thrust lines. Snipers working in pairs were to target enemy vehicle commanders forcing them to close down.

**Forces** operating in the OZ were to take the momentum out of enemy attacks and to separate the infantry from supporting armour, groups of four to six soldiers equipped with radios, anti-tank weapons and supported by heavy or light armoured fighting vehicles were to engage in shoot and scoot tactics.

Defending its sector, "nowhere to go . . . ." - Delay zone of combat

**On** reaching the DZ, for tactical reasons certain road and rail bridges were to be demolished. Before demolishing military engineers would liaison with civil authorities to turn off water, gas and power supplies. Infantry pioneers and combat engineers regularly practised the laying of explosives on the bridges.

**In** the DZ, streets and roads were to be blocked by demolishing buildings, erecting barbed wire obstacles and utilising available materials. Anti-tank mines, booby traps and anti-personal mines were to be laid to force the enemy into areas where one - three street ambushes had been prepared.

Defending its sector, "nowhere to go . . . ." - Yellow pages

**With** the nature of urban combat, a high casualty rate was expected especially in the OZ and DZ. Evacuation of casualties to the combined Allied Hospital with APCs would be unrealistic due to streets being blocked by rubble, mined, or swept by enemy fire. In the FDZ medical teams were to come forward.

Units in Berlin familiarised themselves with the Berlin-Yellow pages telephone books as a source of information to where building materials and plant equipment could be obtained to construct obstacles and defensive positions in the Brigade's Combat Zone (BCZ).

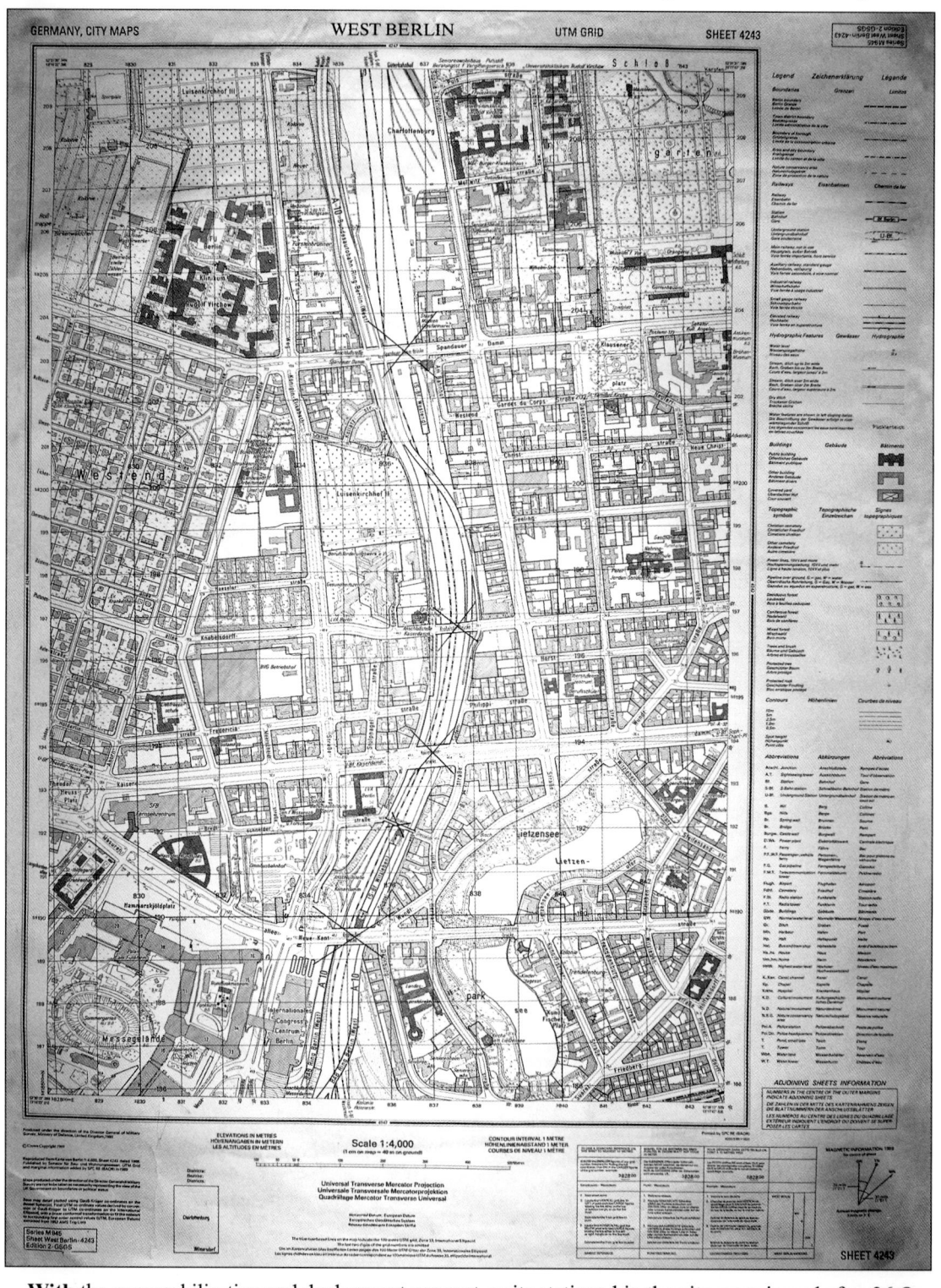

**With** the new mobilisation and deployment concept, units stationed in the city were issued after 26 October 1982 with Berlin Mobilisation Mapping Packs by 14 Topography Sqn RE. Each pack contained 3 x 4 sheets per set from the War Office, Geographical Section General Staff, map series M945, 1:25,000 and 18 sheets from the 1:4,000 map series. The battalions were each issued with seven Mapping Packs, the other units ranging from one to four Mapping Packs.

Defending its sector, "nowhere to go . . . ." - Final defence zone of combat

**The** Final Defence Position (FDP): a prepared position where mutually supporting companies in Bastions fight the final defensive battle with all remaining sources. The Bastions were to be prepared as defensive positions incorporating false fronts, and alternative positions with obstacles, wire and mines.

**It** was expected that by the time combat had reached the FDP, infantry battalions would have suffered heavy casualties. Battalions were to be reinforced with uncommitted logistic troops, to fight in an infantry role. Reserves were to be held but, because of the small area to be defended only of significant size.

Defending its sector, "nowhere to go . . . ." - Lessons learnt

The FIBUA report from 1982 pointed out that the standard British northern hemisphere camouflage netting, green and brown, was unsuitable for urban combat. The report suggested that a dual-purpose camouflage netting be developed and introduced with one side for vegetation and the reverse for urban environment.

With the new defence strategy, trials highlighted that the Brigade's recoilless light infantry anti-tank weapons systems, L6-Wombat, L14A1-Carl Gustav Infantry Gun and Milan (later LAW 80) if fired from a confined area such as a room, could result in serious injury or the killing of the gun crew, if not carefully positioned.

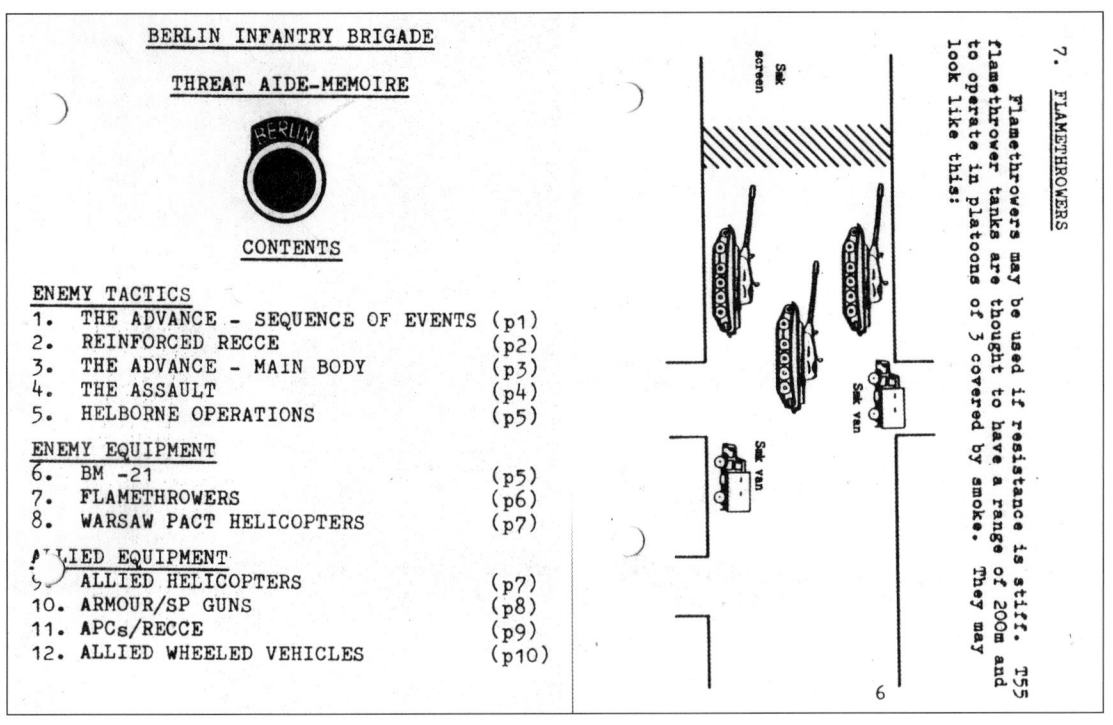

Defending its sector, "nowhere to go . . . ." - Lessons learnt

```
        BERLIN INFANTRY BRIGADE
           THREAT AIDE-MEMOIRE

                  CONTENTS

ENEMY TACTICS
1.  THE ADVANCE - SEQUENCE OF EVENTS  (p1)
2.  REINFORCED RECCE                  (p2)
3.  THE ADVANCE - MAIN BODY           (p3)
4.  THE ASSAULT                       (p4)
5.  HELBORNE OPERATIONS               (p5)
ENEMY EQUIPMENT
6.  BM -21                            (p5)
7.  FLAMETHROWERS                     (p6)
8.  WARSAW PACT HELICOPTERS           (p7)
ALLIED EQUIPMENT
9.  ALLIED HELICOPTERS                (p7)
10. ARMOUR/SP GUNS                    (p8)
11. APCs/RECCE                        (p9)
12. ALLIED WHEELED VEHICLES           (p10)
```

7. FLAMETHROWERS

Flamethrowers may be used if resistance is stiff. T55 flamethrower tanks are thought to have a range of 200m and to operate in platoons of 3 covered by smoke. They may look like this:

**Pocket** Threat Aide-Memoire first issued in July 1982 were distributed at section level to junior non-commissioned officers. Following recommendations from the regiments, the packs were updated in 1983 to include Soviet and Warsaw Pact armoured fighting vehicles and helicopters.

**The** shoot and scoot tactics relied on speed. The FIBUA report from 1982 recommended that the combat order tactical webbing equipment, enabling a soldier to survey 24 hours in the field, should be enhanced with a small rucksack for the carrying of extra ammunition which would be needed in urban combat.

Defending its sector, "nowhere to go . . . ." - Workshops' role

**With** an expected 20 minutes of heavy artillery barrage before the start of a ground offensive, the deep cellars in the city would give protection to regiment, headquarters and the Brigade's workshops. The joint Allied headquarters was to be in an upgraded World War Two air raid shelter, below Wilmersdorf Town hall.

**Before** deploying to the cities's cellars. The workshops were to make maximum use of their static facilities and skilled manpower to restore as much key equipment as possible to battle-worthy condition, within the time frame imposed by the state of alert and the requirement to abandon their base.

Defending its sector, "nowhere to go . . . ." -Workshops' role

**In** the OZ and DZ phases of battle, the Light Aid Detachment workshops, attached to the battalions and armoured squadron, were responsible for first line repairs. Second line repairs were to be back loaded to the Royal Electrical and Mechanical Engineers (REME) workshops deployed at Olivaer Platz.

**When** combat had reached the FDZ armoured vehicles, which were unmovable due to engine failure, were to be hauled into positions determined by their commanders and used as static firing points, pill boxes.

Defending its sector, "nowhere to go . . . ." - Battle tanks in FIBUA

At a briefing given by Major C.D. Daukes of D-SQN 4/7 DG on 3 March 1982, he emphasized the advantages and disadvantages of the Chieftain tank in an urban battle. Two of the points raised, were the one meter maximum climbing capability of a Chieftain and that only one tank in Berlin had been fitted with a dozer blade.

The Major added that the ammunition for the still fitted 0.5 Machine Gun (MG), which had been withdrawn with the introduction of the LASER rangefinder system, be reissued as the 0.5 MG which could fire exploding rounds would be an excellent weapon in urban warfare against enemy soft bodied vehicles and infantry.

Defending its sector, "nowhere to go . . . ." - Urban camouflage

**Prior** to the FIBUA report from 3 March 1982, the armoured fighting track driven vehicles deployed in Berlin were painted in the standard British Northern European theatre camouflage, green and black. The report recommended that a new camouflage be considered for vehicles operating in urban warfare.

**To** comply with the report, the vehicles were painted in an urban camouflage comprising of grey, white and brown symmetrical forms which blended into an urban environment. The camouflage was unique to the British track driven vehicles deployed in Berlin.

Defending its sector, "nowhere to go . . . ." - Logistic in FIBUA

# LOGISTIC IN FIBUA OPERATIONS

## THE BERLIN LIBUA STUDY-WINTER 1981/82

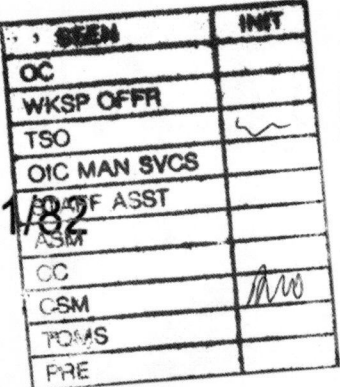

J E J LANE
Lt Col
DCOS G1/G4

**The** study of logistic support in urban war, Logistic In Built UP Area (LIBUA), from 3 March 1982 pointed out that the general war method of supply and re supply was unsuitable for FIBUA because the distances involved in the Brigade Combat Zone, were from the start of the Obstacle Zone to the rear of the Final Defence Zone less than 5 kilometres. In addition, after enemy bombardment, numerous streets would be blocked with rubble and later may be crated and mined or swept with enemy direct fire. It added that normal re supply under these conditions would incur unnecessary casualties to men and equipment.

Defending its sector, "nowhere to go . . . ." - Dumping to task

**The** LIBUA study recommended that a system of forward dumping to task should be established in the three combat zones. These would offer a mixture of combat supplies, especially ammunition, anti-tank ammunition, explosives and mines. With careful dumping the time taken for units to draw supplies would be reduced.

**The** report added that supporting arms such as the armoured units, combat engineers and infantry pioneers, due to the nature of their task should be re supplied separately, adding that the dumping of mines and explosives into working areas must have a high priority in all three combat zones.

## Royal Air Force Gatow.

**Under** the terms agreed for the division of Berlin into four Allied sectors, the British were to inherit the former German Airfield at Gatow. The unit tasked with taking over the airfield from the Soviets was No. 2848 Sqn RAF Regiment, which arrived in Gatow by road from Magdeburg on 25 June 1945. The handover was less than amicable with the Squadron being held virtually prisoner behind barbed wire in hangar No. 1 for several days for arriving "too early".

The unit initially became 19 Staging Post and the first entry in the Air Traffic Control log book was on 2 July 1945. In retaliation for the delays imposed by the Soviets on the overland transit route checkpoint at Marienborn, the RAF at Gatow withdrew refuelling and repair facilities for Soviet long range aircraft. On one occasion in the summer of 1946, Andrei Vyshinsky from the Soviet Foreign Ministry spent the day drinking two bottles of vodka at the airfield while the Marienborn checkpoint was being "unblocked".

The cause and general history of the Berlin Airlift are widely documented. As the British airhead, Gatow was from the start heavily involved and the operation has been called the Station`s "finest hour".

Activity at Gatow decreased after the Airlift. In July 1951, RAF Gatow was put onto a care and maintenance basis. By November 1951 strength was down to 12 officers and 50 airmen.

During the early 1950s the airfield was frequently "buzzed" by Soviet aircraft. However on 23 October 1952 one Mig 15 made an unscheduled landing in error at Gatow, but managed to escape by taking off from the grass apron, chased closely by the station's fire engine and the station's commander in his private car.

On the 21 April 1953, seven civilian internees released by North Korea passed through Gatow, en-route to Britain. The aircraft, a Hastings of Transport Command, had flown to Moscow with a Soviet signaller and navigator aboard. The released party included a journalist, three high-ranking clergymen, and three diplomats, one of whom was the Soviet master spy George Blake.

April of 1963 saw a dramatic incident: The television personality Hughie Green, who was coming to Gatow to present his television show (Double Your Money), had requested permission to fly a Cessna directly to Gatow from Stuttgart via the Southern air corridor. Mr. Green entered the corridor and was immediately followed by two Soviet Migs, both aircraft made several close passes rocking their wings and lowering their under carriages. Mr. Green held his course and height. Shortly before entering the Berlin Control Zone, the Migs on six occasions opened fire from behind and 200 feet to the left of the Cessna. Mr. Green subsequently landed safely at Gatow.

The highlight of 1965 was the Royal visit on 27 May. The Queen and Prince Philip landed at Gatow on the occasion of the state visit to Berlin. A very popular addition was added to the station`s facilities on 5 July 1969:- a nine hole golf course. In 1970 two Sioux helicopters of 7 Army Aviation Flight were deployed to Gatow, who set up their base in No. 3 hangar. On 6 May of the same year, the first new WRAF contingent arrived to serve on the station. These were the first airwomen to be base at Gatow since the post-Airlift run down (in 1990 there were 62 WRAF at Gatow).

On 9 April 1978, two young East German brothers made an unauthorized landing at RAF Gatow in a Zlin 42m. The brothers were handed over to the Berlin authorities and the Zlin was later returned to the East Germans via Glienicker Bridge. During the same month, a Handley Page Hastings No. TG503, a veteran of the Airlift, made its final journey to the grass apron at the main gate where it took up position as gate guard. An East German glider piloted by Wolfgang Seiler landed at Gatow on 24 June 1979. After debriefing, he was handed over to the refugee reception centre at Marienfelde and the glider was returned to the East Germans on 28 June. An RAF Hercules aircraft landed in February 1981 with a fuel leak in No. 4 engine. After investigation a bullet hole was found in the air frame along with a 6mm steel core, the latter indicating to non-Western origin. On 26 May 1987, Queen Elizabeth II flew to Gatow to attend the Queen`s Birthday Parade. The controllers in the Air Traffic Control tower spotted on 15 July 1987 a light aircraft with East German markings approaching the airfield. The aircraft landed and was surrounded. The pilot had used the occasion of his second solo flight to defect. He was debriefed and handed over to the civil authorities.

In 1990 the first signs of the changing political situation in Germany came into effect. A German military aircraft landed at Gatow for the first time since 1945: On 11 October a Bundeswehr BO 105 helicopter came in to refuel. At a ceremony on 30 June 1994, the airfield was officially handed over to the German Air Force.

Royal Air Force, Gatow - The early days

**Gatow** airfield was built in 1934-35 for the needs of the German Air Force Flying Training School and the School of Air Warfare. The airfield fell to the Soviets on 26 April 1945 and the British took control on 4 July 1945. A detachment of 284 RAF Regiment, who had arrived two days earlier, were detained by the Soviets.

**On** 1 August 1945, what had been known as RAF Unit Berlin became Royal Air Force Station Gatow. Up to this time, Gatow had been a grass airfield. Sappers from the Royal Engineers began on 8 August 1945 to lay a 1325-yards-long runway of Perforated Steel Planking (PSP). In 1947, a concrete runway was added.

Royal Air Force, Gatow - Finest hour

**The** Soviets in a bid to drive the Allies out of Berlin, closed on 24 June 1948 the overland routes between the western zones and West Berlin, on a pretext that the river Elba bridges were unsafe and needed repairs. Access to the city from the west was reduced to the air corridors, guarantee in the 1945, Air Corridor Agreement.

**The** British were first to respond to the Soviet's blockade with Operation Plainfare. The first aircraft carrying food landed at RAF Gatow on 25 June 1948. Three days later, the RAF in a 24 hour operation delivered 44 tons in 13 Dakotas. Air Commander Waite, calculated that 1,534 tones of provisions and fuel were required daily.

Royal Air Force, Gatow - Finest hour

**Until** permanent quarters could be arranged, the extra 269 soldiers and airmen, posted to Berlin to support the airlift, were first bivouac at Gatow airfield adjacent to the runway and unloading aprons.

**To** mess the extra military and civilians working at Gatow, the Army Catering Corps set up temporary field kitchens next to the unloading aprons. Before the airlift, the transit mess at Gatow was serving 220 meals daily. During the airlift this increased to over 3,500 meals.

143

Royal Air Force, Gatow - Finest hour

**The** RAF having tanker aircraft flew into Berlin the petrol, oils and liquids. To transport the fuels from the airfield, pipelines used in WWII, Pipe Lines Under the Ocean (PLUTO), were brought from Britain and at first laid overland. The first pipeline became operational on 5 December 1948, the second in March 1949.

**Military** and civilian teams were responsible for unloading the aircraft. The transporting of the supplies into the city was undertaken by the West Berlin haulage company of Harry W. Hamacher, known to all as Honest Harry. For his efforts Mr. Hamacher was made a honorary member of the Berlin British Legion.

Royal Air Force, Gatow - Finest hour

**With** the constant starts and landings, the concrete runway at Gatow required resurfacing. With no raw materials available, Royal Engineers cannibalised the ballast stones from railway tracks in the western sectors along with bitumen from bombed streets. The resurfacing was completed on 16 July 1948.

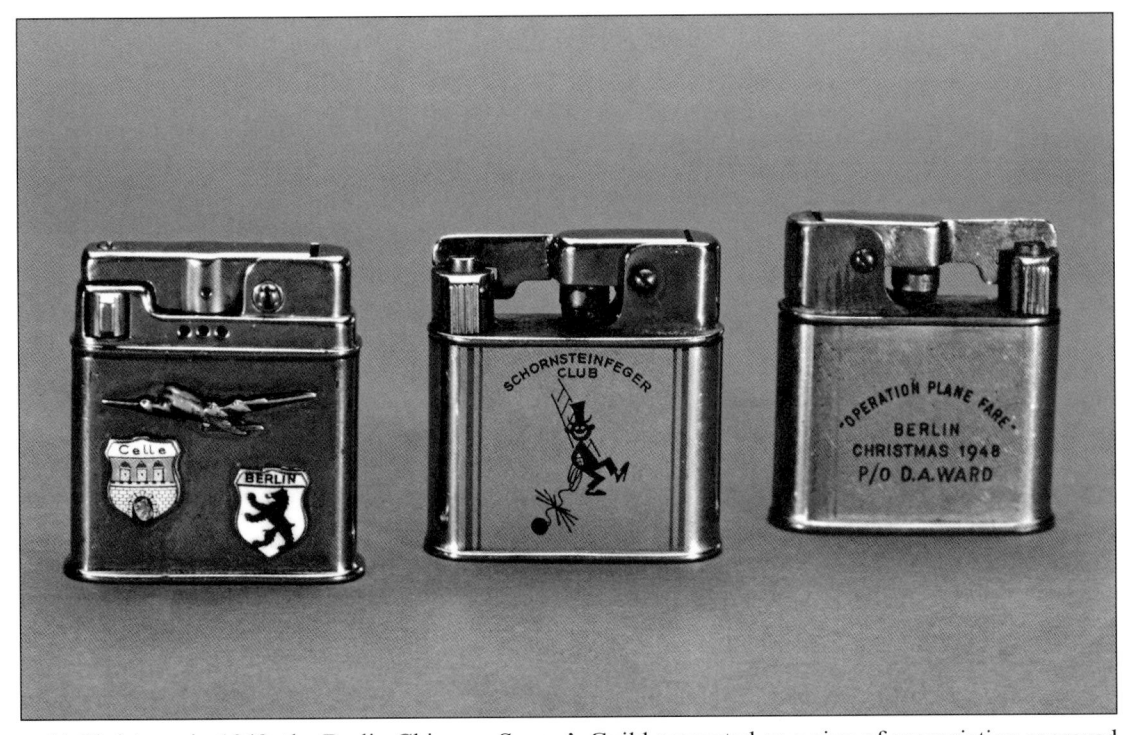

**At** Christmas in 1948, the Berlin Chimney Sweep's Guild presented as a sign of appreciation engraved cigarette lighters to the British aircrews who flew into Gatow. The guild wrongly misinterpreted the operation name and had plane instead of plain engraved on the lighters.

Royal Air Force, Gatow - Finest hour

**With** the ever increasing tonnage being flown. At the beginning of 1949 the Allies were delivering up to 7,000 tons of freight and fuel daily. In the face of increasing adverse criticism through out the world, the Soviets realised that they had failed to archive their objective and started to seek a face saving solution.

**Following** negotiations at the United Nations, the blockade was lifted on 12 May 1949. The Allies continued flying supplies into the city until 6 September 1949. With the last aircraft landing at Gatow, a total of 277,726 flights had been made by Royal Air Force and charted British civil aircraft.

## Royalty come to Berlin.

**At** the height of the Cold War Her Majesty Queen Elizabeth II and her husband, The Duke of Edinburgh (Prince Philip), visited West Berlin on 27 May 1965 as part of a four day state visit to West Germany. It was the first visit by a British monarch for over half a century. Up to this visit, British sovereigns had officially ignored Germany. During her short stay in the city, she reviewed the troops at the annual parade held in her honour, inspected the Berlin Wall in front of the Brandenburg Gate and gave a speech at Rathaus-Schöneberg.

Visitations to the Brigade and Berlin by British royalty fell into three categories: official, private and state. The Queen's visits to the city coincided with state visits to West Germany, and were organised and managed at government level as part of her state duties. Her visits to Berlin were used by the British Government to focus international attention on the Berlin situation and to demonstrate to the Berliners that the British Government stood behind its commitment to safeguard the freedom of the city against communist aggression. The Guard of Honour for state visits was provided by the three Western Allied garrisons. Official visits to the Brigade and to the city were made by members of the royal house-hold such as Princess Anne or Prince Charles and lasted from one to three days. Visits followed a standard program: inspecting a unit, looking over the Berlin Wall at the Brandenburg Gate, lunching with the Governing Mayor, which included signing the city's golden book, if they had not so at a previous visit, and finally a ball in the evening at the British Officers Club. The Guard of Honour for such visits was drawn from the duty battalion.

Private visits by the royal family to inspect regiments stationed at the garrison of whom they were Colonel-in-Chief or to attend an event as the Brigade's guest of honour such as the Tattoo were low key occasions with little pomp.

Most visits, official, private or state, were timed to allow the royal guest to take the salute at the annual Queen's Birthday Parade or to promote British sponsored events. Regardless of what royalty was visiting, for the soldiers involved it was extra duties and at least one week of "spit and polish".

In the seventies and eighties, for one reason or another, a steady flow of British royalty came to the city. Prince Charles made three visits to Berlin, on 20 October 1972 and on 7 June 1985 representing the Queen at the Brigade's QBP. At his second visit, he also inspected the Gordon Highlanders as their Colonel-in-Chief. On his third visit on 24 March 1992, he attended the Brigade's draw-back parade.

Princes Anne's first of four visits to the Brigade was on 6 June 1973, when she viewed an army school and the Berlin Wall. In 1984 and 1988, she represented her mother at the QBP, inspected the Armoured Squadron as Colonel-in-Chief and observed a house-to-house clearing demonstration at Ruhleben Fighting City. On her fourth visit in September 1990, she was guest of honour at the British Military Concert "Bandanza" held at the Waldbühne open air theatre. The Duke of Edinburgh came to Berlin on 7 February 1984 to open a British trade exhibition and give a speech at a reception to local business representatives at Charlottenburg Palace. Princess Margaret made a 24 hour visit to the Brigade on 23 May 1986 and was scheduled to take the salute the following morning at the QBP. But due to what was described by the Commandant as a "headache", the British Ambassador to West Germany took her place on the rostrum.

As part of Berlin's 750th anniversary, the Queen came to the city from 26 to 28 May 1987. As with her previous visits, she attended the annual QBP. In September 1992, she made a state visit to the now unified Germany. As part of her schedule she unveiled a plaque at the site of the old and new British Embassy in East Berlin and laid a wreath at the Brandenburg Gate in memory of East Germans killed trying to escape into the west. In the evening she was guest of honour at a performance of the last Berlin Military Tattoo.

In an attempt to squash speculation in the British and international press of a rift in the couple's marriage, Their Royal Highnesses, The Prince and Princess of Wales, Charles and Diana, visited Berlin from 31 October to 2 November 1987 and attended as part of the Berlin's 750th anniversary celebrations the performance of the London Royal Ballet Company at the West Berlin opera house on Bismarck-Strasse. Prince Edward made a short visit to the RAF at Gatow in 1988 to open the new terminal building. The Duchess of York, known to all as "Fergie", made a four day visit to Berlin from 25 to 28 May 1989, where she drove a single-deck bus, inspected the Brigade's logistic support units and the troops at the QBP.

Having officially no royal family, the British royalty were enthusiastically received by the Berliners and the local press.

Royalty comes to Berlin - Royal standard

**During** the British occupation, Her Majesty Queen Elizabeth II's Royal Standard was hoisted on Charlottenburg-Palace for the duration of her visit to the city. The Queen has visited Berlin on four occasions: 27 May 1965, 24 May 1978, 26/27 May 1987 and after unification on 2 October 1992.

Royalty comes to Berlin - Queen's Birthday Parade

To celebrate the coronation of Queen Elizabeth II, a parade was held at the Maifeld in Berlin on 5 June 1953. Thereafter it became an annual event in May to celebrate the Queen's official birthday (coronation) and was known in the British military events calendar as the Queen's Birthday Parade (QBP).

The Queen coincided her visits to enable her to take the salute at the Maifeld birthday parade. To avoid an air incident, the Soviets grounded all military flights in the region until the aircraft carrying the Queen had cleared the Berlin air corridor.

Royalty comes to Berlin - Royal visitors

In her absence, the Queen was represented by a member of the Royal Household who inspected the troops and took the Royal Salute at the march pass. The Royal Salute at the last QBP on 19 May 1990 was taken by Princess Alexandra. Prince Charles, attended a farewell parade at the Maifeld on 27 May 1994.

Queen Elizabeth, The Queen Mother in her role as Colonel-in-Chief, made a private visit on 1 July 1987, to the Black Watch Regiment. She returned on 17 March 1990, to present her annual gift of shamrock to the Irish Guards on Saint Patrick's Day, during her visit she inspected the remains of the Berlin Wall.

Royalty comes to Berlin - Colonel-in-Chief

**Princess** Anne, as Colonel-in-Chief of the 14th/20th Royal Hussars, visited B Squadron in May 1988. A hands-on demonstration was organised at Ruhleben training complex by the squadron for the British and local press.

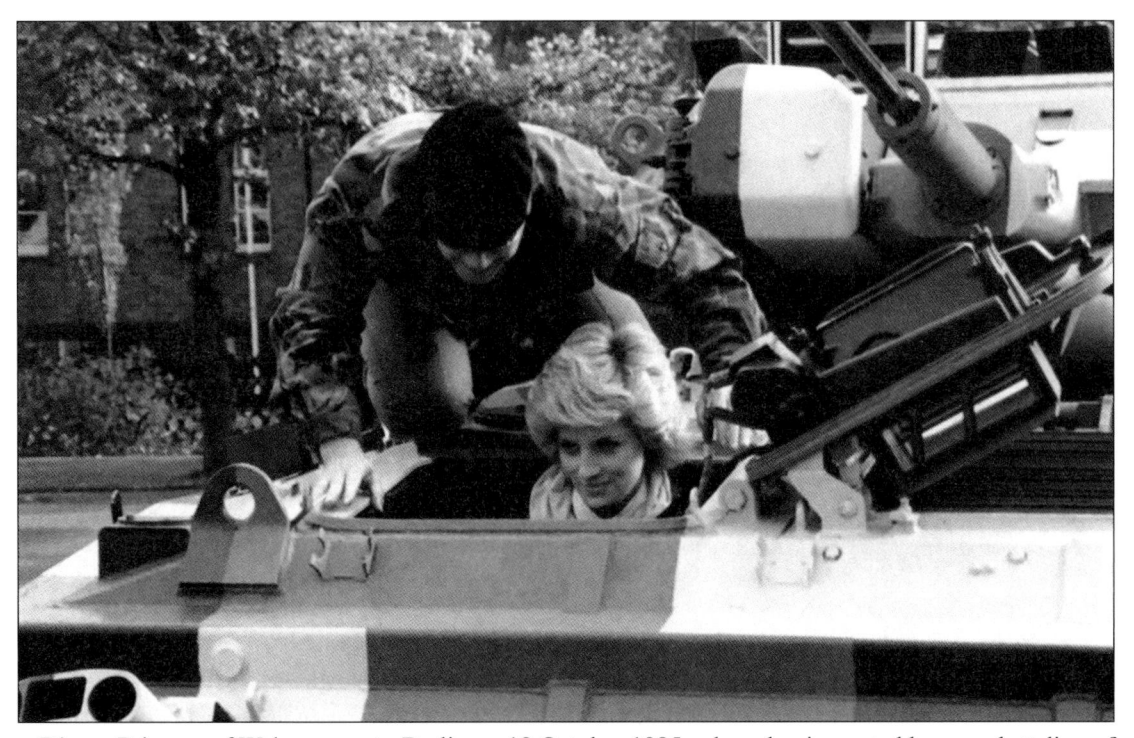

**Diane**, Princess of Wales, came to Berlin on 18 October 1985, when she inspected her own battalion of the Royal Hampshire Regiment, whose Colonel-in-Chief she had been since June. She retained the honour until her divorce and the withdrawal of her royal privileges in 1996.

## Brigade's Infrastructure.

**Responsibility** for the procurement and allocation of all accommodation required by British Forces in Berlin was centralised in British Headquarters and was exercised in accordance with the procedures outlined in the Berlin Area Plan. Within the headquarters the responsibility was performed by G-4, through its Property Service and Engineers sub-sections. Although assignments of areas within the sector, as indicated in the revision to the First Key Plan, were changed considerably in the actual occupation, methods of requisitioning properties for accommodation were generally carried out as planned. After the arrival of the Preliminary Reconnaissance Party on 1 July, the Royal Engineers immediately opened a Property Service and Labour Office at Wilmersdorf Town Hall, later to become Lancaster House. One of its principal duties was the surveying, requisitioning and registering of all properties required by British Forces in the sector, within the limitations imposed by G-4 as to the properties and areas assignments. The properties established by the Berlin Area Plan according to users were: British Military Government Headquarters, medical installations, quarters for combat and service troops, perishable-supply depots and welfare institutions (clubs, canteens, etc.).

Written requests for specific properties or general accommodation by the prospective users, who were forbidden to make reconnaissance of property without G-4 approval, were submitted to British Headquarters and processed by the accommodation sub-section of G-4 to assure conformity with housing plans. Upon approval by G-4 the requests were forwarded to the Engineer Property Service and Labour Office for assignment of the required property. Formal requisitions, if not already made, were then accomplished by that office through the Military Government and the Bürgermeister (Mayor) of the municipal district in which the property was located. Other authorised methods of procurement were seizure of property of direct military value with the possibility of later payment and confiscation of property of the Reich (former German central government), NSDAP (Nazi Party) and subsidiary agencies of either. Characteristic for the control exercised by British Headquarters was the statement of policy, made immediately after the entry into Berlin, that it was responsible for the selection and block allocation of property for all British Forces in the sector.

The position of British Headquarters, as the principle service and supply agency for all British Forces in Berlin coupled with the difficulties imposed by Berlin's isolation, required it to provide a number of large installations for service, receipt, storage and issue of supplies. One of the largest of these was the quartermaster depot handling Class I, II and IV supplies, which was installed in a former Wehrmacht barracks at Rauchstrasse in Spandau. Originally selected only by map reconnaissance, the installation was found to possess rail lines, sidings and storage capacity adequate for all needs.

The allocation of properties as billets for British Forces in Berlin with an average strength of approximately 25,000 constituted a task of comparable magnitude to that of providing space for head quarter offices and service installations. Within the areas assigned by G-4, units largely composed of enlisted men were generally housed in existing military barracks or large blocks of apartment buildings, although office buildings and industrial factories had to be used in some cases. Close grouping was practised in order to facilitate command, security administration and communications, as directed by the British Area Plan. In tactical units such groups were usually of battalion size. The service units as a rule were handled similarly and when possible were billeted in or adjacent to the installation which they operated.

As a result of aerial bombing or house to house fighting, practically every important building or residential area requisitioned by the British Forces had suffered some degree of destruction. Further damage had occurred because of improper care or the looting indulged by Soviet soldiers. Although responsibility for the repair and maintenance of accommodation rested with the unit to which they were allotted, the technical direction, supplies and equipment, required in setting up an unusual number of large installations in a serviceable condition, placed the burden of rehabilitation in the British sector on the Engineers. It was the opinion of the Engineers, that many of the deficiencies of personnel, and material first experienced in Berlin could have been avoided if the Engineer Staff had initially contained fifty percent more older and higher ranking officers with a background in municipal engineering. The engineering troop list, originally comprising 1,300 men, should have been 4,500 men and made up of special construction, utilities, depot and maintenance units rather than combat engineers and assault pioneers.

Brigade's infrastructure - Barracks

**Brooke** and Wavell Barracks, took their names from Field Marshals Brooke and Wavell. Situated at Wilhelstadt, Brooke's entrance was on Seeburger-Strasse and Wavell's on Schmidt-Knobelsdorf-Strasse. Until the British withdrawal in 1994 they were the homes of two of the three infantry battalions stationed in Berlin.

**Montgomery** Barracks, on Sakrower-Land-Strasse, took its name from Field Marshal Montgomery. Built in 1935 for the German Air Force Signals Wing, it fell to the Soviets in April 1945 who handed it over to the British on 12 July 1945. From 1945-1994, it was the home to various infantry battalions.

Brigade's infrastructure - Barracks

**Smuts** Barracks, named in 1945 after Field Marshal Jan Smuts was situated on Wilhelmstrasse. Stationed at Smuts were the Brigade's engineering support squadron (RE) and armoured contingent who from 1945-1954 were based at MacKenzie-King (Canadian Prime Minister) Barracks on Berkaer-Strasse in Wilmersdorf.

**Alexander** Barracks, situated on Hohenzollernring, was named after Field Marshal Alexander. Originally named Schulenberg-Kaserne, it had been built in 1877 for the Prussian Army. From 1945-1994 the barracks had been continuously occupied by the garrison's transport squadron and supporting workshops.

Brigade's infrastructure - Villa Lemm, Edinburgh House

**The** British Commandants residence in Berlin from 1945 to the unification of Germany on 2 October 1990 was Villa Lemm on Rothenburg Weg. It was built by the architect Max Weerner in 1907 for the Berlin industrial, Otto Lemm. During World War Two it was occupied by a high ranking member of the NSDAP.

**Designed** by the Berlin architect Werner Duttman, and completed in 1962, Edinburgh House situated on Theodor-Heuss-Platz served until December 1994 as a transit hotel for British Forces. For security, concrete bollards were embedded along the front of the hotel to prevent ramming by terrorist vehicles.

Brigade's infrastructure - Gatow Ranges

**For** small arms live firing the Brigade had two practice areas at its disposal: the training complex at Ruhleben and a 600 metres facilities at Gatow. In 1985, local Gatow residence took a unsuccessful legal action to the House of Lords in London to stop the building of the ranges at Gatow.

**A** detachment of the Small Arms School Corps was responsible for the organisation, safety and maintenance of the ranges. The use of the facilities was not restricted to the Brigade. The Americans, French and the Berlin Police Force, although having their own ranges, frequently used the British facilities.

Brigade's infrastructure - British Military Hospital

The 84th British Military Hospital, was responsible for the garrison's medical and dental care. It was first located in the Police Barracks on, Land-Strasse in Spandau. In May 1967 it moved to the newly built hospital on Dickensweg. Beneath the hospitals main building was a NBC shelter with wards and operating theatres.

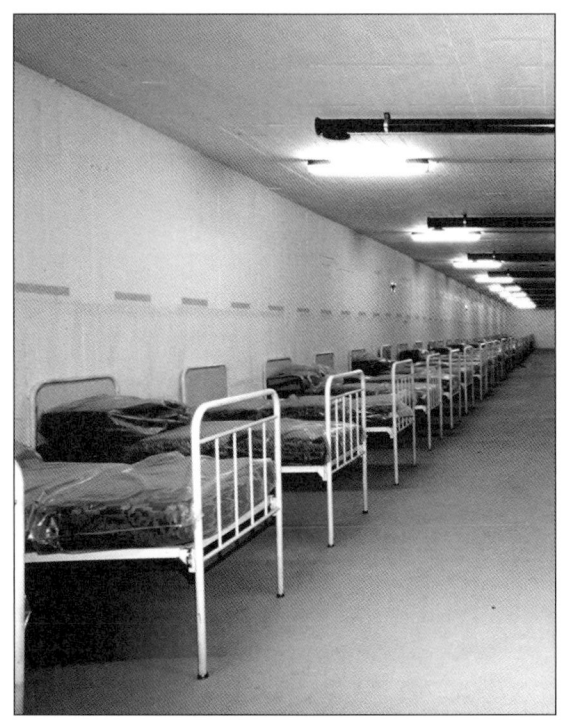

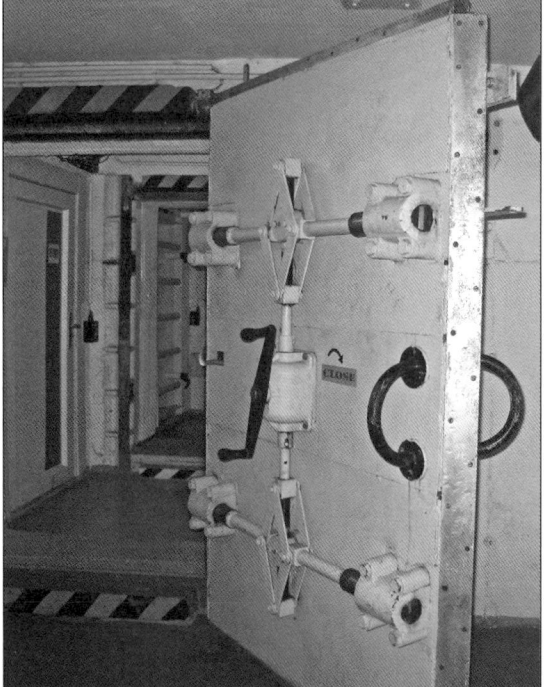

In the event of war the hospital was to be abandoned and moved to the joint Allied Hospital. Soldiers unfit to fight were to be side loaded to local Berlin civilian hospitals. The rest were to be returned to their units as fit to fight. The hospital closed in June 1993 as part of the Brigade's draw down program.

Brigade's infrastructure - Navy Army Air Force Institute (NAAFI Club)

**The** building on the then named Reichskanzler-Platz, renamed Theodor-Heuss-Platz in 1963, which the Navy Army Air Force Institute (NAAFI) requisitioned on 9 October 1945 for their Berlin club, was the former Amerika-Haus built in 1929-31. As a result of an Allied night air raid on 23 November 1943, the building required considerable repairs. With a shortage of building materials in Berlin, the NAAFI engineers obtained permission to roam the city and cannibalise from former government buildings any building materials they needed. The insulating slabs for the refrigerating rooms came from Sachsenhausen concentration camp. In the 750 seat theatre the stage equipment came from the Kroll-Opera-Haus, which after the burning of the Reichstag in 1933, had become the seat of the German parliament.

Brigade's infrastructure - Navy Army Air Force Institute (NAAFI Club)

**Marble** for the entrance came from Göhring's Air Ministry and von Ribbentrop's private residence, the balcony from the Foreign Office and the Reichschancellery. The front doors cannibalised from the Gestapo offices on Van-der-Heydstrasse, the kitchen, central heating and water equipment from the Officer's Messes.

**After** ten months of rebuilding by 600 workmen and women, the now named Summit House was officially opened on 1 August 1946 as the NAAFI Club Berlin by the Marshal of the Royal Air Force, Sir W. Sholto Douglas GCB MC DFC, Commander-in-Chief British Forces-of-Occupation-in-Germany.

Brigade's infrastructure - Berlin war cemetery

**In** the World War Two Graves Commission Cemetery on Heerstrasse are the graves of servicemen from Britain, the Commonwealth, Poland, prisoners of war who died in captivity or on the notorious forced marches and eight unknown servicemen who lost their lives in World War Two.

**After** taking control of its sector, the remains of the British servicemen who were murdered at Sachsenhausen Concentration Camp to the end of World War Two, and those who had died in Prison of War Camps, were recovered and buried at the cemetery with full military honours.

Brigade's infrastructure - British Berlin Yacht Club

**Opened** in 1946 as the United Forces Sailing Club, renamed in 1952 the British Berlin Yacht Club, the club provided sailing facilities to all ranks and mooring for the RE heavy ferries. A West German terrorists group detonated an explosive device at the club on 2 February 1972 killing the club's boats man Herr E. Beelitz.

**During** the Airlift the club temporarily became Gatow Marine Base. The jetty was used by barges to ferry the cargos of salt from the RAF Sunderland aircraft which landed on the Havel Lake. The fuel pipelines, PLUTO, from Gatow airfield had their pumping and distribution terminals at the club's harbour.

## Brigade's infrastructure - British Forces Broadcasting Service (BFBS)

**The** forerunner to the British Forces Broadcasting Service (BFBS) was the British Forces Network, which was established in London in 1943 by the Ministry-of-Defence. With the end of the hostilities in Europe, the London studios closed and moved on 29 July 1945 to Hamburg in the British zone.

**The** Hamburg studios moved on 31 December 1953 to Cologne. It was not until June 1961 that the now named BFBS started to transmit from studios in Berlin. These were first housed at Smutts Barracks, and in 1967 at Summit House. On 18 September 1990, the studios moved to the Britannia Centre in Spandau.

Brigade's infrastructure - St. George's church, St. George's Hall

**The** garrison church, St. George's, on Baden-Allee served the Brigade's religious community from 1953 as a multi-denomination place of worship. On Sunday mornings the church's religious status changed within the hour, the chaplains were provided by the Royal Army Chaplain's Department.

**For** social events St. George's Hall on Scott-Weg was available. Above the entrance was the Berlin brigade's shield. It was one of two locations where the shield was mounted on a building. The other being above the entrance of the Berlin Infantry Brigade Headquarters, London Block at the stadium barracks.

Brigade's infrastructure - British Centre, Toc-H club

**To** promote British culture and arts, an information centre was first opened at Lehniner-Platz in 1949. The newly formed in 1957 British Council took over the scheme and opened premises at Lietzenburger-Strasse. In 1961 the council moved to Hardenberg-Strasse where it remained until 1994.

**The** Toc-H Club at 61 Schönwalder-Allee was opened by two English ladies on 1 September 1945. The club's mobile canteen sold hot tea, sticky buns, newspapers, Playboy and Mayfair magazines disguised in brown paper bags. The wagon was a welcome site at morning NAAFI breaks.

## *"Immediately"*, 9 November 1989.

**On** the morning of 9 November 1989, political and military analyst could not have predicted that before the day ended the political face of Europe would have dramatically changed and the beginning of the end of the Cold War, which would eventually lead to the collapse of the Warsaw Pact. In his speech on 19 January 1989 the East German leader, Erich Honecker, predicted "the Wall, will still be standing in 50 or 100 years time". By 18 October, Honecker had been toppled from power by Egon Krenz and his Wall prediction was starting to show deep cracks.

In the summer of 1989, dramatic political changes were sweeping through Eastern Central Europe. Hungary had opened their borders with Austria and Poland had a democratic free elected government. Following a visit to East Berlin by the Soviet President Mikhail Gorbachev on 7 October, when, in his historical speech, he openly warned Erich Honecker to heed the changes that were taking place in Central Europe or risk political isolation, weekly Monday protests started. At first, in Leipzig where 100,000 took to the streets demanding free elections and freedom of travel. For fear of becoming isolated and unable to stop the increasing unrest, which had now reached Berlin, Krenz's government in an attempt to keep control had little choice but to meet the protesters' demands.

At a the end of a televised press conference on 9 November 1989, Herr Schabowski, the East German government spokesman, gave details of revised travel arrangements which would permit East German citizens unrestricted travel including West Berlin and West Germany. Riccardo Ehrman, a journalist employed by an Italian news agency, asked when the new arrangements would take effect. Schabowski replied that as far as he could make out, it would take effect immediately.

East Berliners hearing of the news gathered in their tens of thousands at the border crossings, demanding that they should be permitted to cross to West Berlin. The border guards manning the crossings, aware of the new travel arrangements, but unsure of the situation and unable to contact their superiors, raised the barriers and stood aside. The first East Berliners came through Checkpoint Charlie at 2120 hours. Hearing the news through the media that the Wall was open, West Berliners and the world press converged at the Brandenburg Gate. In defiance of the East German border guards, West Berliners climbed the two-meter-high wall and sat on top of it. In the following days, the Allies were unable to forecast the political events which were to take place in East Germany and Moscow's reaction to the situation.

After an initial period of uncertainty and evident concern at the time, the Soviets proposed talks at ambassadorial level. These took place on 11 December 1989 at the Allied Control Council building at Kleistpark in West Berlin. Honecker's prediction, like Hitler's thousand-year-Reich, fell short of its mark.

*"Immediately"*, 9 November 1989 - Major General Corbett at the Wall

**To** obtain a first hand account of the events at the Brandenburg Gate, Commandant Maj. Gen. R. Corbett visited the area on 10 November 1989 and spoke to the Berliners. The previous evening he had informed the Soviet guards at the Soviet war memorial that he had personally taken responsibility for their safety.

**At** the opening of the Wall at Potsdamer-Platz in November 1989, East Berliners crossing into West Berlin were greeted by young British soldiers from the 1st. Battalion King`s Regiment, who to help stem off the cold November weather served them with British military style tea, hot and sweet.

*"Immediately"*, 9 November 1989 - Hammers and chisels

**Within** hours of the opening of the Wall, souvenir hunters armed with hammers and chisels started to chip the Wall away. The amount of Wall which was sold to tourist, as genuine Berlin Wall, would have encircled the city at least twice. Segments with interesting graffiti work were auctioned off by the city at an auction held in Monaco in 1990, to museums and art collectors.

*"Immediately"* - 9 November, 1989 - Opening of the Brandenburg Gate

**On** the evening of 22 December 1989, two pedestrian crossings were opened at the Brandenburg Gate. After 28 years of denial by the Soviet backed East Berlin Government, Berliners, east and west, took the opportunity to walk through the Gate's archways.

**Work** began on 19 February 1990 to dismantle the now porous Wall. Sappers from 38 Fld. Sqn. RE assisted in dismantling the Wall and watchtowers along the British/Soviet zone border in Spandau. A number of Wall segments eventually found their way into British and Commonwealth museums.

## Re-unification - The Draw down.

**1990** was the most important year for Europe and Germany since the foundation of the Federal Republic in 1949. As the year began, the socialist system based on denial of freedom and oppression, had collapsed in East Germany. German unity was no longer a dream but an expectation, distant at first but rapidly moving from likelihood to reality. In mid-February, an agreement was reach on a "2+4" forum for negotiations between the Four Powers, East and West Germany on the external aspect of establishing German unification. On 18 March, the first free elections were held in eastern Germany for nearly fifty years. The Christian Democratic Union Party with its stand for rapid unity won the election. The result was seen as reflecting the will of the people of East Germany to unite with the Federal Republic by way of accession. In the meantime, Berlin, a powerful political symbol, was beginning to merge together as one city.

On 1 February, Allied traffic started to cross into the Soviet sector via the checkpoints at Invalidenstrasse in the British sector and Bornholmer-Strasse in the French sector, in addition to using the only previous crossing Checkpoint Charlie at Friedrichstrasse. After an approach to the Soviet Embassy in East Berlin on 27 April, all sector border crossings were open to Allied travellers. In a move aimed at updating the image of the British administration in Berlin, the British Military Government was renamed the "British Mission Berlin". On 4 May, the Band of the 1st Battalion the Light Infantry with the Drums and Pipes of the 1st Irish Guards was the first British military band to perform in East Germany (Soviet zone) at Werder. The British Deputy Commandant referred to the military band as "our secret weapon".

The re unification of Germany saw the retention of the British Army and the other military forces occupying Berlin. Under the terms of the "2+4" Agreement the British Government was asked by the German Government to keep their troops in the city as guarantors of this agreement until the final withdrawal of Soviet Union Military Forces from German soil. Between 2 October 1990 and the end of September 1994, the most significant aspect of this period was the change of status that took place on unification.

The Berlin Stationing Agreement, between the Federal German Republic, the United States of America, France and the United Kingdom, signed in September 1990, was the document that determined how British Field Forces garrisoned in Berlin would operate after unification. The agreement permitted the garrison to continue its training in Berlin and that the German authorities would continue to finance the Brigade under the Berlin Defence Costs Budget. The fundamental change arose from the fact that the British troops became subject to German Law and that the Military Police would no longer enjoy special status in the city.

Re-unification saw a number of instant changes. Until the unification of divided Germany, the special rights and responsibilities provided for the post-war governing of Berlin and which were vested in the person of the three western Allied Commanders in the western Sectors of the city, lapsed automatically, as it were. Hence the requirement for the Generals and their ministers to depart on 3 October 1990. The Allied Staff Berlin closed, their reason d`être having disappeared with the events of 9 November 1989 and the deployment of the Bundeswehr in Berlin, which had been prohibited since the end of World War Two. Thus from 1990, there were military elements from five nations present in the city. Unification did not mean the beginning of the end of the British presence within the city.

The garrison had four years to plan and conduct their draw down. The first two years of unification saw the closures of a number of organisations that had been essential to the running of the Brigade when it had been an isolated community: the Headquarters and Signals Regiment disbanded in January 1991, the military train ran for the last time in February of that year, the Helmstedt RMP post closed in March, and the British Military Hospital closed in May. The following year saw the draw down gather momentum with the closure of Teufelsberg in February, the departure of 2 RMP in June and the farewell to the last British armoured squadron in Berlin, C Squadron 14/20 Hussars and the 1st Welsh Fusiliers in August. By 1992, the overall strength of the Berlin Field Force had reduced considerably with the Brigade consisting of only infantry battalions and Royal Air Force Gatow reduced by 50%. By this time, the major units in the city were the 1st Battalion the Gordon Highlanders, who departed the city in spring 1993, and the 1st Battalion Queen`s Lancashire Regiment, who withdrew a year later.

After nearly fifty years presence in Berlin and having seen the last piece of unfinished business of 1945 completed in a manner that many viewed as impossible only months before the actual events, the British packed their bags and officially withdrew from their sector in September 1994.

Re-unification - 2+4 Agreement

**With** the collapse of the communist system in East Germany and the election of a democratic forum, the question of a German unification was first raised at a meeting in Ottawa on 13 February 1990. The re-unification question could only be resolved with the consent of the Four Occupying Powers.

**With** the signing of the 2+4 Treaty in Moscow on 12 September 1990 by the Foreign Minister of the Occupying Powers and representatives of East and West Germany, the occupational status of Berlin ceased. It was agreed that the Allies would remain in Berlin until Soviet troops had left German soil.

Re-unification - Goodbye Charlie

With the new political situation in Berlin, the Allied Checkpoint Charlie (C) on Friedrichstrasse had become obsolete. At a ceremony on 22 June 1990, attended by military and political representatives of the Western Allies and ministers of the two Germanies, the checkpoint was officially disestablished.

A group of 118 artists from 23 countries converged in 1990 at the inner border Wall on Mühlen-Strasse and painted murals depicting past and present political events associated with the Wall and the opening in November 1989. This length of rear Wall, named East Side Gallery, has become a tourist attraction.

The draw down - A museum to the Allies

**The** German Chancellor Helmut Kohl proposed in 1991 a museum to document the Western Allies presence in Berlin. At a press conference on 24 July 1994 attended by the Brigade Commanders Yates, Brullard and Bromhead, requisites were handed over to the museum as a symbol of Allied support.

**Unique** to Berlin was the British urban camouflage pattern which the Chieftain battle tanks, the AFV430s and AFV432s were painted in. The museum was presented with an AFV432, minus engine, night sight and fitted with a piece of pipe representing the 30 mm RARDAN cannon.

The draw down - A museum to the Allies

A reconnaissance vehicle, AFV 701 MK 1/2, Ferret Scout Car, similar to the vehicle which for propaganda had escorted a young school boy from his home in the Eiskeller in Spandau to school, was handed over to the museum. The boy falsely claimed in 1961 that he had been harassed by East German border guards.

**Requisites** linked to the British occupation, such as uniforms, military equipment, documents and Tattoo items, were donated to the museum by the Brigade.

# PARADE
### der Alliierten Streitkräfte in Berlin
18. Juni 1994 10.00 – 12.00 Uhr · Straße des 17. Juni
Zwischen Charlottenburger Tor und Kleinem Stern

**THANK YOU MERCI DANKESCHÖN**

At the farewell parade on 18 June 1994, hosted by the Berlin Senate, the governing mayor of Greater Berlin, Eberhard Diepgen, thanked the Western Allies in the name of the people of Berlin for having sustained from 1945 to 1990 the freedom of two million inhabitants in the western sectors of the city.

The draw down - Everyone has a suitcase in Berlin

**The** Allied withdrawal from Berlin in the summer of 1994 was similar to the first months of occupation in 1945, with numerous parades and presentations. Major differences were the Soviets absence and the presence of representatives of the German Armed Forces.

**After** 49 years of presence in Berlin and having successfully completed a 3 year draw down program, British troops official withdrew from the city on 8 September 1994. A rear party stayed on until the end of December 1994 to finalise the hand-over of buildings to the German authorities.

## British Commandant and General Officer Commanding, Berlin Area 1945 to 1990.

**From** the first Commandant, Major General L. O. Lyne, July - September 1945, to the last, Major General R. J. S. Corbett, 16 January 1989 - 2 October 1990, 21 British officers held the post. On average the posting was for two years and was a combined military and political appointment.

Major General
L. O. Lyne CB, MC
July 12 - September 1945

Major General
E. P. Nares CB, CBE, MC
September 1945 - May 1947

Major General
E. O. Herbert CB, CBE, DSO
May 1947 - January 1949

Major General
G. K. Boume CB, CBE
January 1949 - October 1951

Major General
C. F. C. Coleman CB, DSO, OBE
October 1951 - March 1954

Major General
W. P. Oliver CB, OBE
March 1954 - May 1955

Major General
R. Cottrell-Hill CBE, DSO, MC
May 1955 - February 1956

Major General
F. D. Rome CB, CMG, CBE, DSO
March 1956 - March 1959

Major General
Sir R. Delacombe KBE, CB, DSO
April 1959 - May 1962

Major General
C. I. H. Dunbar CB, CBE, DSO
May 1962 - December 1962

Major General
Sir D. Peel-Yates KCB. CVO, DSO.
December 1962 - January 1966

Major General
Sir J. Nelson KCVO, CB, OBE, MC
February 1966 - February 1968

Major General
F. J. C. Bowes-Lyon OBE, MC
March 1968 - November 1970

Major General
The Earl Cathcart CB. DSO. MC
November 1970 - July 1973

Major General
D. W. Scott-Barrett
August 1973 - November 1975

Major General
R. M. F. Redgrave MC
November 1975 - January 1978

Major General
R. F. Richardson CVO, CBE
January 1978 - September 1980

Major General
J. D. F. Mostyn CBE
September 1980 - October 1983

Major General
B. C. Gordon-Lennox CB, MBE
October 1983 - December 1985

Major General
P. G. Brooking CB, MBE
December 1985 - January 1989

Major General
Sir R. J. S. Corbett CB
January 1989 - October 1990

## Commander.

### Area Troops Berlin (1950 to 1953) Berlin Independent Brigade (1953 to 1959)
### Berlin Infantry Brigade Group (1959 to 1963)
### Berlin Infantry Brigade (1963 to 1977 and 1981 to 1994)
### Berlin Field Force (1977 to 1980).

| | | |
|---|---|---|
| Brigadier D. R. Morgan, DSO, MC. | March 1950 - | May 1952. |
| Brigadier F. Stephens, DSO. | May 1952 - | October 1953. |
| Brigadier F. W. Sandersons, DSO, ADC. | February 1954 - | October 1955. |
| Brigadier M. W. Roberts, CBE, DSO. | October 1955 - | October 1958. |
| Brigadier G. J. Hamilton, CBE, DSO. | October 1958 - | October 1961. |
| Brigadier R. H. Whitworth, MBE. | October 1961 - | December 1963. |
| Brigadier A. M. Taylor, MC. | December 1963 - | November 1966. |
| Brigadier D. J. M. Tabor, MC. | November 1966 - | November 1968. |
| Brigadier R. W. L. McAlister, OBE. | November 1968 - | August 1971. |
| Brigadier P. A. Downard, DSO, DFC. | August 1971 - | July 1974. |
| Brigadier L. A. H. Napier, OBE, MC. | July 1974 - | June 1976. |
| Brigadier C. R. Grey, CBE. | June 1976 - | June 1978. |
| Brigadier T. N. McMicking. | June 1978 - | June 1980. |
| Brigadier J. A. Evans. | June 1980 - | June 1982. |
| Brigadier A. Makepeace-Wame, MBE. | June 1982 - | December 1984. |
| Brigadier P. P. D. Stone, CBE. | December 1984 - | December 1986. |
| Brigadier R. F. Powell. | December 1986 - | December 1988. |
| Brigadier R. A. Oliver, OBE. | December 1988 - | December 1990. |
| Brigadier D. de G. Bromhead, LVO, OBE. | December 1990 - | September 1994. |

## Deputy Commandant and Minister,
## 1961 to 1990.

| | | |
|---|---|---|
| Mr. G. L. McDemott, CMG. | July 1961 - | July 1962. |
| Mr. A. G. Rouse, CMG, OBE. | July 1962 - | September 1964. |
| Mr. P. T. Hayman, CMG, CVO, MBE. | October 1964 - | September 1966. |
| Mr. R. G. A. Etherington-Smith, CMG. | October 1966 - | March 1970. |
| Mr. J. W. C. Bushell, CMG. | April 1970 - | December 1973. |
| Mr. J. H. Lambert, CMG. | January 1974 - | May 1977. |
| Mr. F. R. McGinnis. | June 1977 - | February 1983. |
| Mr. D. J.. Wyatt, CBE. | March 1983 - | October 1985. |
| Mr. M. E. Burton, CMG, CVO. | November 1985 - | October 1990. |

## Roll call of British units that served in Berlin, 1945 to 1994.

| | |
|---|---|
| The Life Guards. | LG. |
| The Blues and Royals (Royal Horse Guards and 1st Dragoons). | RHG/D. |
| 1st The Queen's Dragoon Guards. | QDG. |
| The Royal Scots Dragoon Guards ( Carabiniers and Greys). | SCOTS GD. |
| The Royal Dragoon Guards. | 4/7 DG, 5 INNIS DG. |
| The Queen's Own Hussars. | QOH. |
| | |
| 3rd The King's Own Hussars. | KOH. |
| The Queen's Royal Irish Hussars. | QRIH, 8 H. |
| 9th/12th Royal Lancers (Prince of Wales). | 9/12 L. |
| The King's Royal Hussars. | 11 H, RH, 14/20 H. |
| The Light Dragoons. | 13/18 H. |
| Royal Tank Regiment. | 1 RTR, Indep Sqn, 4 RTR. |
| | |
| Royal Regiment of Artillery. | 6 Tp 46 AD Bty. |
| Corps of Royal Engineers. | 38 Fd Sqn, Postal and Courier. |
| Royal Corps of Signals. | Berlin Sig Regt, 13 Sqn. 229 Sqn. |
| Grenadier Guards. | 1 & 2 GREN GDS. |
| Coldstream Guards. | 1 COLM GDS. |
| Irish Guards. | 1 IG. |
| | |
| Welsh Guards. | 1 WG. |
| The Royal Scots ( The Royal Regiment). | 1 RS. |
| The Royal Highland Fusiliers ( Prince Mageret's Own). | 1 RSF, 1 RHF. |
| The King's Own Scottish Borders. | 1 KOSB. |
| The Black Watch ( Royal Highland Regiment). | 1 BW. |
| Queen's Own Highlanders ( Seaforth and Camerons). | 1 QO HLDS. |
| | |
| The Gordon Highlanders. | 1 GORDONS. |
| The Argyll and Sutherland Highlanders ( Princess Louise's). | 1 A & SH. |
| The Prince of Wales's Royal Regiment. | 1/5 QUEENS, 2 QUEENS, 2 RWK, 1 R HAMPS, 7 HANTS. |
| The Royal Regiment of Fusiliers. | RNF, 1 RF, 2 & 3 RRF. |
| The Royal Anglian Regiment. | 1 NORFOLKS, 1 R LINCS, 2 NORTHANTS, 2 ESSEX, 1 E ANG, 2 & 3 R ANGLIAN. |
| The King's Own Royal Border Regiment. | 1 BORDER, 1 KOB. |
| | |
| The King's Regiment. | 1 MAN, 1 KINGS. |
| The Prince of Wales Own Regiment of Yorkshire. | 1 E YORK, 1 POW. |
| The Green Howards (Alexandra Princess of Wale's Own). | 1 GREEN HOWARDS. |
| The Queen's Lancashire Regiment. | 1 S LANCS, 1 QLR. |
| York and Lancaster Regiment. | 1 Y & L. |
| The Royal Irish Regiment 27th (Inniskilling) 83rd, 87th and the Ulster Defence Regiment. | 1 RIF, 1 INNISKILLING 1 & 2 R IRISH. |
| | |
| The Devon and Dorset Regiment. | 2 DEVONS, 1 & 5 DORSETS. |
| The Cheshire Regiment. | 1 CHESHIRE. |

| | |
|---|---|
| The Royal Welsh Fusiliers. | 1 RWF. |
| The Royal Regiment of Wales 24th/41st of Foot). | 1 WELCH, 1 RRW. |
| The Cloucestershire Regiment. | 1 & 2 GLOSTERS. |
| The Worcestershire and Sherwood Foresters Regiment (29th/45th of Foot). | 1 WORCS, 1 WFR. |
| The Stafford Regiment ( The Prince of Wales). | 1 STAFFORDS. |
| The Duke of Edinburgh's Royal Regiment (Berkshire and Wiltshire). | 1 DERR. |
| The Light Infantry. | 1 KOYLI, 1 & 9 DLI, 1 SCLI, 1 & 2 LI. |
| The Royal Green Jackets. | 1 OX & BUCKS, KRRC, 1 & 2 RGI. |
| The Parachute Regiment. | 1 & 2 PARA. |
| Army Air Corps. | 7 FLT AAC. |
| Royal Army Chaplain's Department. | RACD. |
| Royal Logistic Corps. | RCT, RAOC, ACC, RPC, Postal and Courier. |
| Royal Army Medical Corps. | RAMC. |
| Corps of Royal Electrical and Mechanical Engineers. | REME. |
| Adjutant General's Corps. | ALC, RMP, RAEC, WRAC, RAOC. |
| Small Arms School Corps. | SASC. |
| The Royal Army Dental Corps. | RADC. |
| Intelligence Corps. | INT CORPS. |
| Army Physical Training Corps. | APTC. |
| Queen Alexandra's Royal Army Nursing Corps. | QARANC. |
| Royal Air Force. | Nr. 26 Signals Unit, RAF Provost and Security Detachment. |

## Sources.

Berlin Allied Archive (author), www.berlin-allied-archiv.com
British Army Berlin Standing Orders, Copy Nr.18.
Berlin Bulletin Vol. 35, No. 20. Vol. 36, No. 29, & Vol. 37, No 1.
Berlin and the British Ally, 1945 - 1990, Maj. Gen. Sir R. Corbett, KCVO, CB.
Berlin Brigade FIBUA reports, June 1980 and April 1982.
Berlin Brigade LIBUA report, Winter Studies March 1982.
Berlin Brigade RIBUA report, September 1981 Comd. ( DCOS G1/G4) REME's war role in Berlin
Berlin Brigade Winter Studies - 1 Kings Own Border 26 March 1982.
Berlin Brigade Study - Combat Action of a Soviet Motorized Rifle Battalion in a City.
Berlin Brigade Study - Special to Arm Intelligence Cell (105/10G3), August 1984.
Berlin Brigade Study - Soviet FIBUA tactics 2 March 1982.
Berlin Brigade Study - Winter Studies - D-Sqn 4/7 Dragoon Guards, Use of Armour for FIBUA, 1981.
Bundesarchiv, Germany.
Her Majesty's Stationery Office.
König, Bernd, Berlin, Germany.
Landesarchiv, Berlin, Ehiers, Ludwig.
SLUB Dresden, Deutsche Fotothek, Roger & Renate Rössing.
Spies Beneath Berlin, David Stafford, ISBN 0-7195-6323-2.
Unite States Department of Defence.
United States Headquarters, Berlin District, Report of Operations 8 May - 31 December 1945 Part II.

# Index.

A.
Adenauer, Konrad., 55
Adolf Hitler Platz., 10
Air Corridor., 108, 142
Alexander Barracks., 43, 46, 154
Alexandra, HRH Princess., 149
Allied Forces Day Parade., 19, 70
Allied Commandants., 68, 71, 106, 121, 171, 151
Allied Kommandatura., 19, 58, 62, 63, 73, 169
Allied Military Committee., 65
Allied Staff Berlin., 65, 66, 169
Altglienicke., 94
Annual Report (BRIXMIS)., 85
Armour Division 7th., 13
Armoured Fighting Vehicles (APC's)., 39, 173
Army Air Corps, 7 Flight., 36, 45
Army Catering Corps., 143
Army Corps of Engineers USA., 95
Army Education Corps., 29
B.
Bad Oeynhausen., 112
Base Workshops, REME., 90
Beating of Retreat., 38
Beelitz Herr E., 161
Berlin Airlift., 140, 161
Berlin Area., 8, 9, 26, 152
Berlin Air Safety Centre., 50, 59, 108
Berlin Control Zone., 59, 60, 86, 104, 108, 140
Berlin Document Centre., 54
Berlin Field Force., 23, 125
Berlin Garrison Routine Orders., 30
Berlin Infantry Brigade., 11, 26, 36, 123
Berlin Police., 156
Berlin Senate., 4, 10, 76, 79, 117, 147, 174
Berlin Wall., 75, 99, 101, 121, 147, 167
Bersarin, Maj. Gen., 7
Blake, Gorge., 82, 94, 98, 140
Blake, Rymer., 100
Boume, Major General G. K., 176
Bowes-Lyon, Major General F. J. C., 176
Brandenburg Gate., 5, 16, 40, 52, 117, 121, 147, 165, 166, 168
Brigade Combat Zone., 68, 123, 126, 138
Britannia Centre., 48, 162
British Ambassador., 43, 147
British Armed Forces Special Voucher., 16
British Commandant., 8, 62, 73, 76, 122, 176
British Government House., 10
British Forces., 8, 16, 17, 107, 152, 159, 162, 169
British Military Government., 10, 11, 14, 18, 152

British Military Hospital., 157, 169
British Military Liaison Mission (BRIXMIS)., 85
British Military Train., 19, 112
British sector., 3, 8, 9, 19, 44, 49, 69, 73, 79, 82, 100, 104, 152, 169,
British Travel Directory., 109
British Zone of Occupation., 8, 107
Brooke Barracks., 153
Brooking, Major General P. G., 76, 177
Brullard, Brig., 172
C.
Call Alert., 24, 25
Charlottenburg., 8, 9, 70, 112, 116, 147, 148
Checkpoint Alpha (A)., 4, 42, 110, 111
Checkpoint Bravo (B)., 4, 110, 11,
Checkpoint Charlie (C)., 4, 80, 119, 165, 169, 171
Chief-of-Mission., 83
Churchill, Prime Minister Winston., 13, 18, 50, 53
CIA., 86, 94, 97, 98
Clay, General., 108
Clayton. Reverend P. B. Tubby., 164
Coleman, Major General C. F. C., 176
Colonel-in-Chief., 147, 150, 151
Commonwealth., 7, 53, 160, 168
Control Council., 50, 51, 62, 107, 165
Corbett, Major General Sir Robert., 122, 166, 176, 177
Cottrell-Hill, Major General R., 176
D.
Daukes, Maj. C.D., 136
De Havilland T10 Chipmunk., 86, 88
Declaration of Legality., 3, 7,
Delacombe, Major General Sir R., 176
Delay Zone., (DZ)., 126
Deutschlandhaus., 10
Deutsche Bahn., 114
Devon Regiment, 2nd Battalion., 74
Diane, Princess of Wales., 147, 151
Dohm, Mr. H., 10
Dollis Hill., 96
Dreilinden., 4, 110, 111
Drewitz., 110
Dunbar, Major General C. I. H., 177
E.
East Berlin., 71, 78, 98, 106, 117, - 119, 121, 147, 165, 168, 169, 174
East Germany., 3, 82, 91, 111, 117, 165, 169, 170
East German Government., 92

East German Ministry., 85, 92, 106
E-Mail., 102
East Side Gallery., 171
Edinburgh House., 152
Elizabeth II, Queen., 147, 149
Eisenhower, General D. I., 7, 50, 117
El Alamein., 13
F.
Farewell parade., 75, 149, 174
Federal Republic of Germany., 3
Ferret Scout Car., 173
Fieldstation (Nr.4)., 100
Freisler, Roland., 61
Fighting In Built Up Area (FIBUA)., 19, 123, 125
Final Defence Zone (FDZ)., 126, 129, 135, 138
Four Powers Protocol., 9, 37, 106
France., 7, 33, 50, 56, 61, 62, 169
Freedom of the Borough., 44
Free Hess Organisation., 57
G.
Gatow, RAF., 36, 45, 58, 82, 86, 88, 103, 104, 141-147, 156, 161, 169, 171
Geographical Section General Staff., 130
German Air Force., 41, 141, 153
German Ministry for Air Safety., 61
German Service Unit., 19
German unification., 169
Göhring's Air Ministry., 159
Gordon-Lennox, Major General G., 19, 177
Government Communications., 88, 101
Grade II ration card., 6
Graves Commission., 161
Great Britain., 7, 47, 53, 56
Greater Berlin., 8, 9, 62, 63, 69, 73, 80, 174
Great Patriotic War., 74
Group of Soviet Forces in Germany., 81, 84, 87, 134
H.
Hanns-Braun-Strasse., 11
Hall, James Sgt., 82
Hamacher, Harry W., 144,
Hangar No. 4., 88, 103
Headquarters Berlin Area., 26
Helmstedt., 8, 42, 107, 110, 111, 113, 169
Herbert, Major General E. O., 176
Hertha BSC, 42
Hess, Rudolf., 58
Heuseyin, Yuldirim., 82
Hitler, Adolf., 5, 10, 38, 155
Hohne., 42, 115
House of Lords., 156
Howley. Major General., 64

I.
International Military War Crimes Tribunal., 55, 58
J.
Japan, V-J Day., 54
Jones, KGB CBE. Lt. Gen. Sir Edward., 163
K.
KGB., 82, 93, 94, 98
King`s Regiment 1 Battalion., 166
Khrushchev, Nikie., 118
Kohl, Dr. Helmut., 174
Kroll Opera Haus., 158
L
Lancaster House., 10, 48, 152
Lemm, Otto., 18, 154
Light Aid Detachment., 67, 135
Logistic., 44, 138
Lyne L. O. Major General., 8, 9, 72, 176
M.
MacKenzie King Barracks., 154
Major, Prime Minister John., 11
March and Shoot., 22
March, Werner., 11
Marlinin, Colonel General M., 82, 83
McMicking, Brigadier T. N., 19, 123, 125, 178
Merrell, Major Robert., 100
Military Government Berlin Area., 8, 9
Military Technical Academy., 100
Ministry-of-Defence., 16, 28, 30, 36, 90, 121, 162
Montgomery Barracks., 153
Mobilisation Mapping Packs., 130
Mohnke, Major General., 5
Montgomery, Field Marshal., 7, 52, 62, 153
Mostyn, Major General J. D. F., 177
N.
Nares, Major General E. P., 176
Navy Army Air Force (NAAFI)., 158, 159, 164
Narks., 92
National Volks Army., 85
NBC., 22, 157
Nelson, Major General Sir J., 177
O.
Obstacle Zone (OZ)., 34, 126, 127, 129, 135, 138
Ohrtmann. Franz., 44
Oliver, Major General W. P., 176
Olympic Stadium., 34, 38, 82, 123
P.
PBJOINTLY., 94, 97
Peel-Yates, Major General Sir D., 177
Perring, Sir Ralph., 121
Pipe Lines Under The Ocean (PLUTO)., 144
Plainfair., 144, 145

Plesh, Doc. Janos Oscar., 155
Plötzensee., 61
Potsdam Protocol., 119
Q.
Quadripartie Flight Rules., 59, 108
Queen's Birthday Parade., 19, 81, 147, 149
R.
Redgrave, Major General R. M. F., 177
Reichskanzler-Platz., 10, 158
Reichstag., 5, 75, 122, 158
Ribbentrop, von., 159
Richardson, Major General R. F., 177
Ruhleben Fighting City., 22, 23, 31, 147
Roberts, Major General Sir A., 82, 83
Rome, Major General F. D., 176
Royal Army Chaplain's Department., 163
Royal Welsh Fusiliers. 1st Battalion., 46, 180
Rudow., 94, 97
Ruhleben., 19, 22, 23, 31, 124, 147, 151, 156
Russian Federation., 61
S.
Sappers., 123, 141, 168
Schloss Charlottenburg., 70, 147, 148
Scott-Barrett, Major General D. W., 177
Secret Police., 85, 92, 106
Schönwalder-Allee., 164
Secret Intelligence Service., 82, 94, 97, 98
Sennalager., 42, 115
Sholto, Douglas Sir W., 159
Shoot and scoot tactics., 127
Siegessäule,. 13, 52
Signals., 101, 103, 153, 169, 179, 180
Skill at Arms., 27
School at Arms., 156
Soviet Army., 4, 5
Soviet Commandant., 7, 117, 122
Soviet Military Government., 62
Soviet Military Liaison Mission (SOXMIS)., 83
Soviet sector., 4, 12, 17, 36, 73, 77 - 82, 94, 118
Soviet war memorial., 16, 166
Soviet Zone of Occupation., 4, 8, 9, 107, 108
Spandau., 8, 9, 19, 43, 48, 50, 56, 58, 115, 152, 155, 157, 168, 173
Spandau Prison., 19, 56, 58
Sparks, Les., 96
Speer. Albert., 100
Spy satellite., 99
Stalin, J., 5, 18, 50, 53
Stanley, David., 96
Strasse des 17 Juni., 19, 52, 70, 71, 74, 121
Summit House., 159, 162

T.
Tattoo., 19, 38, 39 - 41, 147, 174
Territorial Army., 30
Teufelsberg, the Hill., 34, 82, 88, 100, 101, 103, 169
The Earl Cathcart, Major General., 177
Theodor-Heuss-Platz., 10, 158
Threat Aide Memoire, 137
Toc-H Club., 164
Topography Sqn RE., 67
Treaty. " 2+4"., 54, 170
Trümmerfrauen., 6
Tripartite., 62, 64-66
Truman, President Harry., 18, 50, 53
U.
U2 Spy plane., 86
Ulbrich, Walter., 118
United Forces Sailing Club., 161
United Nations., 8, 146
Union Flag., 13
V.
Villa Lemm., 18, 159
W.
Warsaw Pact., 3, 4, 21, 24, 30, 82, 87 - 90, 106, 117, 125, 133, 165,
Wavell Barracks., 153
Weapons Meeting., 72
Weeks, General., 108
Weerner, Max., 155
West Berlin., 3, 4, 30, 36, 37, 71, 78,, 93, 117, 118, 123, 142, 144, 147, 165, 166
West Germany., 3, 4, 39, 79, 147, 165, 169, 170, 171
Wolf, General Markus., 82
World Polo Championship., 47
World War Two., 3, 5, 13, 18, 46, 50, 56, 74, 80, 82, 100, 134, 160, 164, 169
Wuensdorf/Zossen., 80, 84, 89, 92
Y.
Yak 28P (FIREBAR)., 104
Yates, Brig., 172
Z.
Zhukov, Marshal G. K., 7, 50, 52, 53, 73, 107, 108

# Chronology.

14.01.1944 - First meeting of the European Advisory Commission, London (UK, US, USSR (France joined on 27 November 1944)).
12.09.1944 - First London Protocol, partition of Germany within 1937 borders into three zones of occupation and Greater Berlin as a "special area" into three sectors.
14.11.1944 - London agreement with Allied decision to establish a Control Council (CC) to administrate occupied Germany. Greater Berlin to be administered by an Allied Kommandatura (AK).
04.02.1945 - Yalta Conference, participation of France in the occupation and control of Germany agreed (Churchill, Roosevelt and Starlin).
28.04.1945 - Soviet Commandant General Bersarin assumes executive power in Berlin with Order No.1.

02.05.1945 - General Weidling signs the instrument of Surrender of German forces in Berlin.
08.05.1945 - Unconditional surrender of Germany, signed at Karlshorst, Berlin.
05.06.1945 - Declaration assuming supreme authority over Germany, and providing legal authority for Allied Control Commission and Kommandatura signed in Berlin.
04.07.1945 - British and American forces officially enter Berlin.

11.07.1945 - The Allied Kommandatura assumes control of the administration of Greater Berlin.
12.07.1945 - Military Government Berlin Area, British take full control over its sector.
16.07.1945 - Mr. Harry S. Truman, President of the United States of America, visits Berlin.
17.07.1945 - The start of the Potsdam Conference (UK. US, USSR - France joined on the 7 August 1945).
19.07.1945 - Visit of the General of the Army, D. Eisenhower, to Berlin.

21.07.1945 - The British Prime Minister Sir Winston Churchill in Berlin.
14.07.1945 - First British /American train arrives in Berlin.
30.07.1945 - First meeting of the Allied Control Council at Kleistpark, Berlin.
02.08.1945 - Signing of the Potsdamer Agreement on political and economic principles for the treatment of Germany.
12.08.1945 - French forces take control of their Berlin sector.

20.08.1945 - The Allied Control Authority opens.
07.09.1945 - Quadripartite parade held on Charlottenburger-Chaussee (in 1953 renamed Strasse-des - 17- Juni) to commemorate Victory over Japan.
17.09.1945 - First licensed newspaper in the American Sector, Der-Tagespiegel.
11.11.1945 - Soviet Memorial to The Great Patriotic War unveiled.
30.11.1945 - Four power agreement reached on air corridors linking Berlin with the western zones.

12.12.1945 - The Berlin Air Safety Centre starts operations.
16.09.1946 - Signing of the Robertson/Malinin agreement.
20.10.1946 - The first free elections in Greater Berlin since 1933 and the last until 2 December 1990.
24.06.1947 - Ernst Reuter, Social Democratic Party, elected Mayor of Greater Berlin.
08.07.1947 - The Soviets veto Ernst Reuter as Mayor of Greater Berlin.

20.03.1948 - The Soviets refuse to cooperate with the Allied Control Council which ceases to function.
16.06.1948 - The Soviets walk out of the Allied Kommandatura, never to return.
20.06.1948 - General Herbert (US) informed the Soviets that the monetary reform would apply to Berlin.
19.06.1948 - The Soviets stop all civilian traffic between West Berlin and the Soviet zone.
24.06.1948 - The Soviets order monetary reform in their zone of occupation and in Greater Berlin.
24.06.1948 - The Western Commanders order the introduction of currency reforms in their Sectors of Berlin (Bank notes had been secretly stored at the British Officers' Club in Haig Barracks, Spandau).

24.06.1948 - The Soviets blockade all land and rail access routes to and from the Allied sectors of Berlin.
24.06.1948 - Operation Plainfare is started by the British.
25.06.1948 - First aircraft carrying food lands at the Royal Air Force Station, Gatow - Berlin.
28.06.1948 - The Royal Air Force fly round the clock and deliver 44 tons of food in 13 Dakotas.
01.07.1948 - British Government introduce ration cards in Great Britain in support of the Berlin Airlift.

15.07.1948 - Royal Air Force starts to fly out from West Berlin civilians and children.
05.08.1948 - Royal Engineers start to construct Tegel airfield in the French Sector.
30.09.1948 - British fly into Gatow a monthly tonnage of 31,788.6 of coal, food, petrol, oils and liquids.
18.11.1948 - Tegel airfield in the French Sector becomes operational.
07.12.1948 - Ernst Reuter is elected Mayor of West Berlin.

20.12.1948 - Western Commandants declare the Allied Kommandatura will resume work.
12.05.1949 - The Soviets end the blockade of the Allied sectors of Berlin.
14.05.1949 - New Occupational Status for West Berlin.
21.09.1949 - Creation of the Federal Republic of Germany.
07.10.1949 - Creation of the German Democratic Republic in the Soviet Zone of Occupation.

07.10.1949 - Berlin proclaimed by the communists as capital of the German Democratic Republic.
10.10.1949 - End of food rationing in Great Britain.
29.08.1950 - The Allied Kommandatura approves a new constitution for West Berlin.
22.01.1951 - The Allied Staff Berlin created.
09.07.1951 - Formal declaration by UK, US and France that the state of war with Germany is terminated.

27.05.1952 - Telephone communications between West and East Berlin are severed by the Soviets.
28.05.1952 - West Berliners are prohibited from visiting the Soviet zone (German Democratic Republic).
05.03.1953 - The death of the Soviet leader Josef Stalin in Moscow.
17.05.1953 - Uprising in East Berlin and in the German Democratic Republic, suppressed by Soviet forces.
25.01.1954 - Start of the Berlin Conference of Foreign Ministers ( Fr., UK, US, & USSR), no progress.

05.05.1955 - The Allied Kommandatura revises the occupational status of Berlin, Declaration of Berlin.
14.05.1955 - Formation of the Warsaw Pact.
20.09.1955 - The Soviets grant full sovereignty to the German Democratic Republic, but retain control over Western Allied movements in their zone.
18.01.1956 - National People's Army is formed in the German Democratic Republic.
28.01.1956 - National People's Army joins the Warsaw Pact.

01.05.1956 - Bundeswehr is formed in West Germany.
22.04.1956 - American/British spy tunnel discovered by the Soviets at Altglienicke/Rudow.
01.03.1957 - Western Allies protest against National People's Army parade in the Soviet sector of Berlin.
27.11.1958 - The Khrushchev Ultimatum (Soviet leader) demanding the Western Allies leave Berlin within six-months.
31.12.1958 - Soviet ultimatum rejected by the Western Allies.

01.01.1959 - Soviets propose a peace treaty with both states of Germany.
04.04.1959 - Live Oak formed to provide external military support to West Berlin as necessary.
13.08.1961 - The Soviets order the East German Government to seal off the Soviet sector (East Berlin) to West Berliners `Berlin Wall´.
19.08.1961 - President J. F. Kennedy sends Vice President Johnson and General Clay to Berlin.
14.09.1961 - Two West German Air Force fighters land at Tegel Airfield, causing a diplomatic incident.
22.10.1962 - The Cuban missile crisis.

22.08.1962 - The Soviet dissolve the Kommandatura in their sector.
17.02.1963 - Mr. Willy Brandt is elected Mayor of West Berlin.
26.03.1963 - The American President J. F. Kennedy visits West Berlin.
07.12.1963 - First issuing of passes by East Berlin authorities allowing West Berliners to visit the Soviet sector and Soviet zone at Christmas.
02.04.1964 - Inaugural flight of direct trooping between Britain and RAF Gatow.

25.04.1964 - First Allied Day Parade held in West Berlin.
12.06.1964 - Soviets and East Germany signed a Treaty of Friendship, assistance and cooperation.
24.09.1964 - Second Berlin Pass Agreement valid for one year allowing West Berliners four separate visits to the Soviet sector and Soviet zone.
06.03.1965 - The British Prime Minister Harold Wilson visits West Berlin.
27.05.1965 - Her Royal Highness Queen Elizabeth II, visits West Berlin.

01.10.1965 - The Allies order the Berlin Senate to introduce a civil defence plan, BKO (6) 11/65.
25.11.1965 - Third Berlin Pass Agreement for Christmas visits.
07.03.1966 - Fourth and last Berlin Pass Agreement for Easter and Whitsun.
06.04.1966 - Soviet YAK 28 aircraft crashes into Steugensee in West Berlin.
30.09.1966 - Albert Speer and von Schirach are released from Spandau Allied prison.

11.06.1968 - East Germany introduces passport and visa requirements on transit routes.
14.02.1968 - Second visit of Prime Minister Harold Wilson to West Berlin.
26.03.1970 - Four Powers Conference at ambassadorial level in Berlin.
12.08.1970 - Soviets and East Germany signed a treaty of non-aggression.
03.09.1971 - The Quadripartite Agreement on Berlin is signed in Berlin.

11.12.1971 - Signing of the German/German agreement over access to West Berlin.
02.02.1972 - Terrorist's bomb exploded at the British Berlin Yacht Club killing one person.
19.05.1973 - Allied Day Parade held on Spandauer-Damm.
18.09.1973 - East and West Germany become full members of the United Nations.
05.07.1978 - The American President Jimmy Carter visits West Berlin.

29.10.1979 - Visit to West Berlin from French President Giscard D`Estaing.
26.12.1979 - Soviet invasion of Afghanistan.
30.10.1980 - The GDR increase compulsory currency exchanges for visitors to the Soviet sector.
10.05.1981 - Dr. Richard von Weizsäcker is elected Mayor of Berlin (West Berlin).
18.08.1981 - Explosive device detonated by terrorists at Andrew-Barracks in the American sector.

11.06.1982 - US President Ronald Reagan visits West Berlin.
29.10.1982 - British Prime Minister Magaret Thatcher visits West Berlin.
25.08.1983 - Explosive device detonated by terrorists at Maison de France, 1 dead and 23 injured.
10.10.1985 - French President Mitterand visits West Berlin.
18.02.1986 - A London court decides against a legal action taken by West Berliners to stop Gatow Ranges.

05.04.1986 - Bomb attack at the discotheque La Belle by terrorists, resulting in the death of three people.
02.10.1986 - Explosive device detonated by terrorists at Spandau War Crimes Prison.
01.01.1987 - Start of celebrations of 750th anniversary of Berlin.
26.05.1987 - Visit to West Berlin from Her Royal Highness Queen Elizabeth II.
12.06.1987 - US President Ronald Reagan visits West Berlin.
17.08.1987 - Rudolf Hess commits suicide by hanging in Spandau prison.
02.05.1989 - Hungary opens its borders with Czechoslovakia.

18.06.1989 - The Last Allied Day Parade.
06.10.1989 - The Soviet leader Gorbachev visits the Soviet sector of Berlin.
06.10.1989 - The last parade of the East German Army (NVA) in the Soviet sector of Berlin.
09.11.1989 - At 2120 hours, the first East Berliners cross into West Berlin.
16.11.1989 - The British Foreign Secretary Douglas Hurd visits Berlin.

02.12.1989 - Summit meeting in Malta between US President Bush and the Soviet leader Gorbachev.
11.12.1989 - Four Ambassadors meeting in Berlin (Fr., UK, US, & USSR).
05.05.1990 - Two + Four talks in Bonn, West Germany.
22.06.1990 - The Allied Checkpoint Charlie (C) on Friedrichstrasse is closed and removed to RAF Gatow.
01.07.1990 - The D-Mark, becomes the common currency in both German states.

01.07.1990 - The treaty between the two states of Germany comes into force.
17.07.1990 - Two + Four Conference in Paris.
12.09.1990 - The final conference and signing of the Two+Four Treaty in Moscow.
02.10.1990 - The Allied Commandants-in-Meeting, meet for the last time.
02.10.1990 - The British Military Liaison Mission, BRIXMIS ceases operations.

02.10.1990 - The Allied Staff is disestablished.
03.10.1990 - Unification of Germany.
03.10.1990 - Departure of the three Western Commandants from Berlin
10.12.1990 - BRIXMIS disbanded.
12.12.1990 - Closing of the Berlin Air Safety Centre.
07.02.1991 - The British Military Train ceases operation.

12.02.1991 - Fieldstation Berlin (Teufelsberg) closes.
22.10.1992 - Her Majesty Queen Elizabeth II visits Berlin.
20.10.1992 - Last British Military Tattoo.
25.01.1994 - The last British armoured vehicles, AFV430 and 432 depart from Berlin.
01.05.1994 - Toc-H Club closes.

30.05.1994 - NAAFI facilities at the Britannia Centre close.
20.06.1994 - Disbandment of 38 Field Sqn Royal Engineers.
30.06.1994 - RAF Station Gatow closes.
30.06.1994 - British Military Berlin Yacht Club closed.
31.08.1994 - The Soviets withdraw from Germany.
08.09.1994 - The Western Allies withdraw from Berlin.
12.12.1994 - Last Radio transmission from BFBS studios Berlin ends with the word, "Tschüss".

## Acknowledgements

I wish to thank the following friends and colleagues for the help they offered in many different ways: Monika Bartzch, Helmut Bruckner, Konrad Butz, my son Sven Duncan Durie, Col. Dr. W. Heinamann, Peter Kauschke, Gerhard Kienbaum for rescuing my external hard drive, Bernd König, Lutz Freundt, Joao Paglione, Prof. Dr. David Stafford, Dirk Ullrich, former soldiers such as Trevor Allison, Sir Robert Corbett for wielding his Staff College red pen, Derick Dobson, John Kean, Chris Robertson and Peter Young all who reminded me of inside information that I had forgotten and my partner Silke.